PERFECT
PHRASES™

for

ESL

Everyday Business Life

PERFECT PHRASES™

for

ESL

Everyday Business Life

Hundreds of Ready-to-Use Phrases That Help You Navigate any English-Language Situation in the Workplace

Natalie Gast

New York   Chicago   San Francisco   Lisbon   London   Madrid   Mexico City
Milan   New Delhi   San Juan   Seoul   Singapore   Sydney   Toronto

The **McGraw·Hill** Companies

3 4 5 6 7 8 9 10 11 12 13 14 15 16 17 18   QFR/QFR   1 9 8 7 6 5 4 3 2 1

ISBN   978-0-07-160838-1
MHID   0-07-160838-9

Library of Congress Cataloging-in-Publication Data

Gast, Natalie.
        Perfect phrases for ESL : everyday business life / Natalie Gast.
             p.   cm.
        Includes bibliographical references.
        ISBN 0-07-160838-9 (Perfect phrases)
        1. English language—Textbooks for foreign speakers.   2. English language—
Terms and phrases.   3. English language—Spoken English.   4. Adult education.

PE1128 .G344   2010
428.3'4—dc22   2009052645

McGraw-Hill books are available at special quantity discounts to use as premiums and sales promotions or for use in corporate training programs. To contact a representative, please e-mail us at bulksales@mcgraw-hill.com.

Contents

Preface: Who Can Benefit from Using This Book?   xi
Acknowledgments   xv

Part 1	**The Global Workforce**	1

Chapter 1	Find a Mentor	3
	Phrases for Finding a Mentor or Obtaining General Help	4
	Phrases for Asking for Specific Help	5

Chapter 2	Observe, Observe, and Then Observe Some More	10
	Phrases to Use When Observing	11

Chapter 3	Ask and Answer Questions and Listen to Others	15
	Phrases to Check Time Availability	16
	Phrases to Check Understanding	16
	Phrases to Clarify Answers	17

Chapter 4	Avoid Saying "In My Country, We . . ."	19
	Phrases Not to Say Unless Asked	20
	Phrases to Say Instead	20

	Part 1 Notes Section	23

Part 2   Small Talk   25

Chapter 5   Interacting in a Small Group   26
 Phrases About the Weather   27
 Phrases About Sports   28
 General Phrases   28
 Ending a Casual Conversation   30
 Phrases to Say Before Pausing   31

Chapter 6   Giving and Accepting Compliments   34
 Phrases Used to Compliment   35
 Phrases Used to Accept Compliments   36

Chapter 7   Giving, Accepting, and Refusing Invitations   39
 Phrases Used to Give Invitations   41
 Phrases Used to Accept Invitations   43
 Phrases Used to Refuse Invitations   43
 Phrases Used to Clarify Invitations   44
 Phrases Used to Buy Time Before Responding
  to Invitations   45

 Part 2 Notes Section   48

Part 3   Using the Telephone   49

Chapter 8   Speak Up and Speak Out   50
 Telephone Listening Practice   51
 Initiating a Phone Call   52
 Phrases to Move Along a Phone Call   53
 Phrases to Get Clarification   54
 Phrases to Close a Phone Call   55
 Phrases to Respond to Telemarketing Phone Calls   56

Chapter 9   Your Voice Mail   58
              Phrases for Recording a Message   58

Chapter 10   Leaving Messages   60
              Phrases for Leaving Messages   62
              Phrases to Use When Taking Messages for Others   62

Chapter 11   Speaking with Someone
              Who Is Difficult to Understand   64
              Phrases to Ask for Clarification   65

Chapter 12   Speaking with Someone
              Who Has Difficulty Understanding You   67
              Phrases to Use When Someone Has Trouble
                  Understanding You   67

              Part 3 Notes Section   69

Part 4   Presenting Yourself   71

Chapter 13   Before You Present   72
              Phrases to Get Information About an
                  Assignment—Content   73
              Phrases to Get Information About an
                  Assignment—Materials   74

Chapter 14   How to Say It   78
              Phrases to Introduce Yourself   78
              Phrases for Emphasis During a Presentation   79
              Closing Phrases   80

Contents

Chapter 15   Answering Questions   82
Phrases If You Know the Answer   82
Phrases for After You Answer a Question   83
Phrases to Clarify Questions   83
Phrases If You Don't Know the Answer   84
Phrases for After a Presentation   85

Part 4 Notes Section   87

Part 5   **Networking Within Your Organization and Beyond**   **89**

Chapter 16   Whom Do You Know?   90
What Is a Network?   90
Phrases to Use Your "Unique-ness" to Your
    Advantage   92

Chapter 17   How to Network   94
What to Do   94
What Not to Do   96
Introductory Phrases to Say   96
Networking Phrases   97
Phrases for Clarification   97
Phrases to Give Opinions   98
Phrases to End a Conversation   98

Chapter 18   Follow-Up   100
Phrases to Further Relationships   100

Part 5 Notes Section   **102**

Part 6   Stress at Work   103

Chapter 19   **What Is Stress?**   105
Phrases to Ask Yourself to Determine If You
     Are Overstressed   106

Chapter 20   **Use the Good Stress**   109
Phrases for Eating Healthful Foods and Avoiding
     Unhealthful Foods   110
Exercising   110
Phrases for Exercising   111
Mental Exercising   111
Phrases to Say to Yourself to Relax   111

Chapter 21   **Lose the Bad Stress**   114
Phrases to Help Reduce Your Stress   114

Part 6 Notes Section   117

Part 7   Directions   119

Chapter 22   **Directions on the Job**   120
Receiving Directions   121
Phrases for Giving Directions to Others   123
Phrases to Use When Taking Directions   124

Chapter 23   **Giving and Following Directions
to Get Somewhere**   127
Phrases to Use When Asking for Directions   128
Phrases to Use When Giving Directions to
     Somewhere   129

Contents

Chapter 24   Other Directions to Consider   131
             Phrases for Directions to Use a New Photocopy
                Machine   131
             Phrases for Directions to Use a New Computer   132

             Part 7 Notes Section   **134**

Appendix A: The American Business Culture in a Nutshell   135
Appendix B: Sports Idioms and Expressions   147
Appendix C: Grammar Notes   151

Who Can Benefit from Using This Book?

Perfect Phrases for ESL: Everyday Business Life is for you if you are a high-intermediate or advanced English as a Second Language (ESL) or English as a Foreign Language (EFL) learner. Learning a language is a lifelong process and learning American English is no exception. When you first began learning English, your need was basic grammar and vocabulary. Your need has now grown to mastering communication skills in order to function in diverse real-life work-related situations.

This book has been created for you if you are living and working, or intend to live, in the United States and join the global workforce with American speakers of English, referred to as Americans in this text. You may travel back and forth between your country and the United States, you may work for a multinational company, or you may work in an American company. You may even be self-employed. You might be in school in the United States or in your country, deciding on a career. In any of these cases, this book will advance your language ability and boost your confidence in expressing yourself in business situations.

Perfect Phrases for ESL: Everyday Business Life will be of value to those in entry-level positions as well as those who have been in the working world for some time. It is intended to help you feel more at ease in job-related experiences in the United States. The phrases offered are not the only phrases you can use, but they give you a starting point on which to build. Write notes in the Notes Sections with new phrases you or others come up with while immersed in specific situations.

How to Use This Book

Perfect Phrases for ESL: Everyday Business Life is organized into seven parts, most of which are divided into several chapters. You may start at the beginning and read through to the end. This is an especially good strategy if you are in your country preparing to come to the United States for employment. This also works if you have been in the United States but are about to **embark on** your first work experience. Work experiences differ greatly from school experiences. You might also choose to use this approach when changing jobs or moving up to a new position within the same company. In these cases, reading through the entire book can give you the ABCs—**Abstract**, Background, Confidence—and put some useful phrases **at your fingertips**.

Of course, you may want to refer to *Perfect Phrases for ESL: Everyday Business Life* on an **as-needed basis**. For example, if you are in a new position that requires a lot of telephone work, turn to Part 3, Using the Telephone. If this is your first trip to the United States and your first time in an American company or the U.S. office of your multinational company, Part 1, The Global Workforce, might be a good place to start.

Remember, this text is designed so you can write notes on the pages following each part. Also **feel free to** underline or highlight sections, **dog-ear pages**, or attach **Post-it Notes**. These memory techniques will help you refer to useful information you may need again. The book is small enough to carry with you in a briefcase or **pocketbook** as a handy reference. Don't be afraid or shy about adding your own phrases and thoughts to the ones already in the book. It is, for example, impossible to anticipate what someone on the other end of the telephone will say. Every situation is unique. Customize this book to your needs.

Idioms and Other Vocabulary

Abstract: summary of important points of a longer text

As-needed basis: refer to only what you need only when you need it

At your fingertips: simple and easily available, handy

Dog-ear pages: to turn down the corner of a page to mark a place

Embark on: start, begin

Feel free to: allowed to, may, not required

Pocketbook: a cloth or leather bag used to hold papers, money, and other necessities, also called a *purse* or *handbag*

Post-it Notes: the trademark name for a small piece of paper that sticks, used for notes

Culture Hints: In many cultures people reading a book or taking an exam start at the beginning and go through in order (A–Z) to the end. In the case of a test, Americans go through and answer what they know first and then they go back to work on what they need to figure out. In the case of a book, unless it is fiction, Americans read what they need to read initially and, often, that is all they read of the book.

Post-it Notes have developed into notes of every color, shape, and size with a sticky back. They are widely used in offices and homes.

Acknowledgments

Andrea Jeszenszky started out as a student with Customized Language Skills Training (CLST) when she came to the United States from Hungary more than twelve years ago. Andi has managed the CLST office and been my right hand for the past ten years. On this project, she became both my right hand and my left, often revealing talents I didn't know she had. I am grateful for her contributions to this book.

I would like to acknowledge my dear friend and companion for more than twenty years, Walter Ladden. In addition to his encouragement, he has brought his superior proofreading and editing skills to this project.

My sincere thanks go to Harriet Diamond, my sister, and Linda Eve Diamond, my niece, for introducing me to the Perfect Phrases series and our agent, Grace Freedson. Linda shared her outstanding support and suggestions. Harriet's invaluable input marks every page of this book. Grace believed in this project and introduced me to McGraw-Hill Publishers. Holly McGuire, my editor at McGraw-Hill, had the knowledge and patience to work with me, a first-time client.

I am thankful to my many friends who believed in me and left me alone to work. Jill Blaufox called at just the right times with encouragement.

Teaching English as a Second Language (ESL) is a giving, sharing, and blessed vocation in which one meets teachers, trainers, and students who leave one with indelible memories. These memories were a great inspiration in writing this book. Thanks to all of you.

Part 1

The Global Workforce

"I Don't Like to Be Alone"

Arturo came directly to our office from the airport, where he had just arrived from Brazil, with his luggage and the statement, "I don't like to be alone." We told him that our initial pre-assessment **pinpointed** his interests and **hobbies**. We said that we planned to send him where he could join others with similar interests. He responded that he meant "not alone from this moment on."

Akira had been here from Japan, without his family, for a month and was going to be here for another five months. The U.S. counterpart of his company anticipated that Akira had fluent English and an outgoing personality. He had neither. Therefore, he was alone much of the time when he wasn't at work and alone and **underused** when at work.

Arturo and Akira were working for the same company. Arturo was in the United States for one month and was staying in a hotel; Akira was here for many months and lived in an apartment, both close to the company. A trainer from my company, Customized Language Skills Training (CLST), was to meet both men the evening after Arturo's arrival at their respective sites for private lessons. I asked the trainer to arrange a meeting with both of them at the hotel lounge, after the lessons, to introduce them and have them speak briefly to each other in English (the only language they had in common).

Arturo and Akira were inseparable from that meeting on. Akira, who had spent much time alone and never indicated it was a problem for him, **thrived** in his new friendship. The gentlemen visited sights in New York City and elsewhere; they shopped in Brazilian shops and Japanese stores and shared cultures with each other. They also traded many business stories, and although they continued with the private language lessons, they also shared some classes. Arturo and Akira formed their own informal mentoring **collaboration**, and after Arturo left the United States, Akira became an informal **mentor** to new arrivals.

The Courage to Ask for Help

Another example of the power of being assertive enough to ask for help is the Jimmy story. Although in a non-business environment, the need was the same and the road to filling it the same—the courage to ask for help. Jimmy, who was from Thailand, was lost in a high school immersion situation; he had done everything he could think of to **fit in**—Americanized his Thai name to Jimmy, wore too-big jeans, untied his name brand sneakers, and had the "right" haircut. Yet he remained an outsider.

He came to our office early for his English as a Second Language (ESL) classes with tears in his eyes. "Natalie," he asked, "don't you think a boy my age needs friends?" There is only one answer to this—yes. "Well, I can't make friends." I asked Jimmy what his hobby was in his country and he said, "Snooker." I asked, "What is snooker?" He described the game—table, sticks, balls, pockets, and so on. "Oh, like pool," I said. He asked, "What's pool?" I found a pool hall nearby and asked a Korean high school football player, the son of a former student, to join Jimmy and me there. Kim and I had never played pool. We all went to the pool hall, and Jimmy took over from there. He taught us how to play snooker. Of course, he won easily. He mentored us, and he felt very good about himself. I hired Kim to meet with Jimmy a few more times to play pool and discuss his own difficulties in fitting in at high school.

Chapter 1

Find a Mentor

What is a mentor, and what can one do to help you and other members of the ever-growing global workforce? A mentor is a person who has the experience to counsel and reassure a less trained, less **seasoned** person—you (the **protégé**).

Some companies offer mentoring programs; others mentor informally through their human resources departments. Some have flexible mentoring situations—a different employee has lunch with the foreign visitor each day of the week—and some leave it up to you, the newcomer, to seek help. Americans often don't know how to reach out to people from other countries on this **quasi**-business quasi-social level. Arturo and Akira—and others—**fostered** their own informal mentoring program. You may have to do the same.

People in the United States are willing to share information and time, but Americans basically value self-sufficiency and independence. They don't always **pick up on** the newcomers' needs. You can build a network around you based on your needs, but it may not be easy. It will, however, help you to maximize your value to the company and the value of the U.S. experience for you. Having a mentoring relationship might increase your chances of a promising career. The first step is to make a list of your needs and update it periodically. Analyze your strengths and weaknesses truthfully. It is in your best interest to be assertive and ask for help.

If you create a more formal relationship with a mentor(s):

- Agree on a schedule of meeting times and **stick to it**.
- Don't rely totally on mentor input; do your own research (Internet, company website, manuals, and newsletters) and share your findings with the mentor(s).
- Consider what you have to offer to the mentor(s) in the way of your knowledge or experience or ideas (e.g., information about customs, taboos, or business protocols in other countries, or your own technological expertise).

Once you **get the ball rolling**, you and your mentor(s), whether formal or informal, will establish a **rapport** and develop a mutually beneficial relationship. If you are in the United States for an extended period of time, you may even **change hats** and become a mentor to another new arrival.

Phrases for Finding a Mentor or Obtaining General Help

Does the company offer a mentoring program?

Do you know how I can find a mentor?

Do you have a mentor in the company?

Whom do you consider a leader in the company? Does he or she mentor anyone?

Could you recommend someone I might be able to help in a reciprocal relationship? I could offer information about my country's culture, market, taboos, and business practices.

Can I shadow that position?

I need guidance.

Would you mind helping me?

*Could you **take me under your wing**?*

I'm eager to learn more about company culture—would you have a moment over a cup of coffee to discuss it?

Your knowledge about [the company, this position] is valuable to me. Are you available to talk about it with me sometime?

I need to ask someone about this.

Would you be the person I should ask?

Do you mind if I ask you about this?

Can you refer me to the right individual?

Where do you think I can get help?

Could you recommend someone in the [computer, sales, bookkeeping, human resources (HR)] department?

Are there any training programs offered by the company that I might join?

Can you suggest some self-study materials or training programs?

*Is there a **lunch and learn** program?*

Phrases for Asking for Specific Help

*Do you know where I can [rent a car, buy **gas**, get a company manual, get help with my computer]?*

Is there a list of [personnel, telephone extensions, contact numbers]?

Is there a company calendar?

Does the company website list company rules?

*Is there **flextime** here?*

Who is the office administrator?

How do I order business cards?

*Whom do I ask about **IT** problems?*

The copier is jammed—whom do I tell about this?

*Is there a [**dress code**, **casual Friday** policy]?*

Where is the washroom?

Are there vending machines in the [pantry, break room, cafeteria]?

Are there assigned parking spaces?

Where is [a good place for lunch, the nearest gas station, a laundromat, a dry cleaners]?

How long is the lunch break?

Do you know where I can [make copies, schedule a conference room, find previous reports]?

Culture Hints: *It is impossible to generalize about an entire country, especially one that is made up of many interacting cultures such as the United States. There are, however, a few characteristics that are generally associated with businesspeople in the United States. American business culture looks favorably upon individualism, initiative, and the competitive spirit. There is an emphasis on individual achievement rather than on collective group efforts.*

Different areas of the United States operate at different speeds. In business, the pace is much faster in the Northeast and the Midwest than in the South and the Southwest. In the Northeast and the Midwest, **as a matter of course**, getting down to business is the rule. There is a minimum of **small talk** until the main order of business is addressed. **Time is money**, A.S.A.P. ("as soon as possible"), **step on it**, and **shake a leg** are expressions that **mirror** the business mind-set in these areas of the country. On the other hand, other areas of the United States move at a much more relaxed pace. In these areas, rushing is considered rude and the "getting to know you" phase plays a bigger role.

Lunch and learn training programs are shorter than full-day or half-day training programs and are presented during a lunch hour or two. Often coworkers present an aspect of their jobs to their fellow employees. By their nature these programs are casual. A **brown-bag** lunch is a small one that you bring—or that the company provides—that can fit into a lunch bag. It usually consists of a sandwich, drink, and snack or dessert.

Idioms and Other Vocabulary

As a matter of course: routine, the usual
Brown bag: a self-packed lunch, food brought from home
Casual Friday: dressing casually on Fridays at work; also called *dress-down Friday*
Change hats: change roles
Collaboration: working together
Dress code: rules about what to wear in a situation or to an event
Fit in: to be accepted

Flextime: a structure that allows employees to work a flexible schedule instead of everyone working a set time (e.g., from 9 A.M. to 5 P.M.)

Fostered: helped develop

Gas: short for the *gasoline* that fuels vehicles and other machinery

Get the ball rolling: start a process

Hobbies: what you like to do in your leisure time, after-work activity (e.g., playing soccer, stamp collecting, dancing)

IT: the abbreviation for Information Technology: using electronic processes for handling information

Lunch and learn: casual **brown-bag** lunches with presenters speaking **off the cuff** on various issues

Mentor: person who has the expertise to counsel a less experienced person

Mirror: copy, imitate

Off the cuff: something said without first thinking about it

Pick up on: notice

Pinpointed: showed the position of something

Protégé: a person who is taught or helped by someone more experienced

Quasi: sort of, partly

Rapport: understanding, agreement between people

Reciprocal relationship: a relationship in which both parties benefit

Seasoned: has a lot of experience

Shadow: to follow a colleague doing his or her job in order to better understand that job and how to perform it

Shake a leg: hurry up

Small talk: talk about unimportant subjects

Step on it: hurry up

Stick to it: keep to the schedule, don't deviate

Take me under your wing: help me, counsel me, guide me
through this [task, process, job]

Thrived: became better

Time is money: indicates how valuable time is in business
(If you waste time, you could lose business and,
therefore, money.)

Underused: not used as much as could be or should be

Chapter 2

Observe, Observe, and Then Observe Some More

You are employed in your position because you are talented in that field of **endeavor**. You may have come to work in the United States for a span of time because you are skilled at what you do and valuable enough to represent your country, your company, and yourself. Your time in the United States will be more productive if you observe everything you see, listen to everything you hear, and ask questions whenever you need to have more information.

What are you observing and how can it best help you? As Sherlock Holmes said to Dr. Watson upon Watson missing a clue in "A Scandal in Bohemia," "You see, but you do not observe. The distinction is clear."

When entering a facility, observe the premises carefully. It will give you clues about the work environment. Look at the parking area, the lobby, the security arrangements, and the reception area, if there is one. Are there private offices and cubicles, or just one large open space? If you enter someone's work space—whether office, cubicle, or desk area—notice the items important to that person, such as diplomas, awards, **plaques**, trophies, family photos, children's draw-ings, and anything else of interest. The more you visually observe your employer, supervisor, manager, coworker, or **subordinate**, the better you will be able to understand that person. The observations that you make will enable you to initiate conversations (**icebreakers**) about that person's interests. In the United States, many people enjoy speaking about themselves.

It is a good idea to have a small pad of paper and a pencil or pen with you at all times to **jot down** questions or information you want to check out later in private. A Blackberry, iPhone, or similar device is a convenient place for notes. You may be in a situation—working **hands-on** with someone—in which you cannot talk or interrupt **on the spot**. Perhaps, something may occur to you **after the fact** and you will want to get back to it. If so, notes can help.

Companies and management styles are unique, just like finger-prints. As there are different cultures in the world, there are different management styles throughout the United States and within specific companies. You will be absorbing a lot of information from many different sources. Therefore, you undoubtedly will have questions or need additional information, especially after observing work-related demonstrations.

Phrases to Use When Observing

Could I see that [one more time, once more, again, more slowly]?

May I watch you . . . ?

I'd like to learn how to . . .

Could you please show me how to . . . ?

What is your preferred method?

Do you mind if I follow along with you?

11

*Is there a **hard copy** of the instructions?*

Could I try this while you are here so you can answer my questions?

I never did this before, but I would like to be able to . . .

***Bear with me**—I'm new at this!*

*Let me try to do that, and, if you think I've got it, I'll be able to **take over**.*

Is there a manual I may refer to in order to learn how this company does that procedure?

Let me write that down so I can do it [on my own, later, after I practice it].

Please repeat that last part and do it more slowly.

I'm sorry, I [don't understand, have a few questions, didn't see it all].

Could you please go over that again?

I didn't catch that—could you repeat what you said?

I think I understand—let me repeat it back to you.

Let me see if I have this correctly . . .

Would you mind helping me?

Could you help me with this, please?

Could you check this for me, please?

Is this what you mean?

Is this how it's done?

Is this how you do this?

Is this [right, correct, how to do it]?

Would you mind reading over what I've written?

What do you think of this draft I've written?

Do you think my e-mail adequately addresses the issues?

Thank you for your patience. I think I [understand, get it, follow] now.

Thank you. Thanks. I really appreciate it.

Culture Hints: *In the United States, especially in the Northeast and Midwest, learning as quickly as you are able to (with the emphasis on* you*) by note taking, independent study, or seizing on training opportunities is admired. Prepare yourself for the challenges of the job.*

There are **myriad** *courses available in and out of the workplace. You have only to open your eyes and ears—and do a little research—to find a course that would be helpful and enjoyable to you . . . and at a reasonable cost.*

English as a Second Language (ESL) instruction is available in every form, at every level. There are intensive, immersion, citizenship, online, and classroom venues. Courses that concentrate on listening, speaking, reading, writing, pronunciation, making presentations, and job-seeking skills are easy to find. Some offerings are free, and others are available at different costs. Americans are very involved in adult education and take courses that range from automobile maintenance and ballroom dancing to computer skills and psychology. There is another advantage to newcomers to the United States. You can take these courses and meet others with similar interests while learning a new skill. Making new friends and **acquaintances** *in a new country is not easy; joining these activities is one way to do that.*

13

Idioms and Other Vocabulary

Acquaintances: people known slightly, less than friends

After the fact: after a situation has occurred

Bear with me: give me some extra time; have patience with me

Endeavor: field of work; effort

Hands-on: learning by doing

Hard copy: information printed on paper from your computer

Icebreakers: things said to make initial conversation more at ease

Jot down: write notes quickly

Myriad: a great number, too many to count, innumerable

On the spot: at the moment it is happening

Plaques: framed awards

Subordinate: person who works under you in a lower position, also called a *report*

Take over: do something that someone else has started; take control

Chapter 3

Ask and Answer Questions and Listen to Others

Never be afraid or shy to ask or answer questions. Questions indicate your intention to do the right thing or help someone else to do it. Therefore, **straighten up**, look the other person in the eye, and appear confident and entitled to fully understand and be fully understood whether you are asking or answering questions. Especially when asking or answering questions, it is important to set up a situation in which you can best be understood. If possible, face the person to whom you are speaking. Do not cover your face or mouth with your hands or with papers you may be holding. Make eye contact to show sincerity and speak slowly and clearly.

Before presenting your clarification question, be **clearheaded** about what information you are looking for. News reporters, who are **immersed** in asking questions and evaluating answers, use question words such as *who, what, where, when, why, how, how much,* and *how many.* It is not enough for you to **pose an intelligent question**, you have to make sure that your question is understood as you intend it to be.

Timing is also important in asking questions and expecting answers. Prior to asking a question that may require discussion time, you should **ascertain** how much time the other person has available.

Phrases to Check Time Availability

When are you available?

Where may we meet?

What does your calendar look like?

*Do you use the **Outlook** calendar on your computer?*

When is convenient for you?

Are you free this afternoon?

Are you [available, free, not busy, open] to [talk, speak, comment, answer a few questions, address this issue] [now, at this time]?

Would [another time be better, later work, you prefer I wait, you want me to call you first, you want me to e-mail you my questions]?

Is now okay? It will only take _____ minutes.

Do you want to discuss this over coffee?

Thank you for making time for me.

Phrases to Check Understanding

Do you understand my [question, meaning, answer to your question, directions]?

Do you understand my [English, accent]?

Do you have any questions about [what I said, what you heard, the project, the work]?

Have I [made myself clear, expressed myself clearly, been clear enough]?

Do you [hear, understand, get] what I said?

Am I speaking [too quickly, too softly, slowly enough, loudly enough]?

Am I using the [correct, right, appropriate, proper] [English, words, vocabulary]?

Did I use the right [idiom, word, words, phrase]?

Do you [hear, understand, get] me?

Should I say that [another way, in other words, differently]?

Do you want me to [clarify, repeat, explain] that?

Should I [say that again, say that in a different way, rephrase that, explain that further]?

I really need this information in order to [do, finish, complete, understand, carry out, accomplish] [the project, the task, the job, the assignment, my work]. (Said when accepting directions.)

I really need you to understand this information in order to [do, finish, complete, understand, carry out, accomplish] [the project, the task, the job, the assignment, your work]. (Said when giving directions.)

Phrases to Clarify Answers

Please [repeat, clarify, rephrase] that.

I didn't [hear, understand, get, catch] that.

Could you say that [again, more slowly, more loudly, in other words, in another way]?

This isn't clear to me—could you go over it one more time? Thank you.

Would you please [explain, demonstrate, show me, tell me, repeat] that again?

Please repeat the [first part, last part].

I think I understand, but let me repeat it back to you.

This is important, so let me be sure I understand you . . .

This is very helpful. So, in other words (summarize) . . .

Culture Hints: *Questioning is discouraged and may be considered rude in some countries. Those people are shy about asking questions; they try to get answers on their own. However, in the United States, many people say, "The only dumb question is the question not asked." It is better to ask a question than act on incorrect information.*

In some cultures looking someone in the eye when speaking is considered as challenging the person. It is thought of as rude. But in the United States, this is not rude; it shows sincerity and attention.

Idioms and Other Vocabulary

Ascertain: find out
Clearheaded: alert, rational, sensible
Immersed: deep in
Outlook: an online calendar program often included in standard office software
Pose a question: ask a question
Straighten up: stand erect

Chapter 4

Avoid Saying
"In My Country, We . . ."

Americans have become curious about and interested in people from other countries and their customs. Therefore, in conversations you have, they will ask you about what you do and how you do it in your country. Those conversations will be enlightening for them and for you.

However, when you are learning about how to perform your work and **time is of the essence**; observe, listen, and learn rather than say, "In my country, we . . ." or "This is how we do it in my country . . ." First, concentrate on what you are being told, shown, and taught; then ask all the questions you may have. Do not presume to correct the systems or processes before you learn them. You may have done things differently and, perhaps, even better in your country. **Nevertheless**, now, you are in the United States, and although your past experience may be most helpful and you certainly will use it, your first step is to learn the current method. Then, you might want to share suggestions based on your experience.

Your coworkers, no doubt, will benefit from your ideas and your example and may incorporate how you perform a task into their thinking with great success. They may find your **outside-the-box** reasoning refreshing. Of course, if you are asked how you worked in the past, then answer.

Phrases Not to Say Unless Asked

In my country, we . . .

This is how we do it in my country . . .

You people . . .

Americans do . . .

I always did it this way [in my country, in my last job, before].

We never did it that way [in my country, in my last job, before].

Why can't I do it the way I always did it?

That doesn't make sense . . .

I don't think your [way, idea, method, plan, system] is going to work.

I like my way better, and I'm [used to, familiar with, accustomed to] doing it like this.

Phrases to Say Instead

Thanks, I'll try that.

I never thought of that.

That could work well.

Good idea. Let me try that.

I'm open to new ideas.

I would be glad to [learn, practice, try] that.

That is new to me, and I'd like to try it.

Thank you for the [idea, plan, information, suggestion].

*That will certainly **streamline** my work.*

What do you suggest?

I'm interested in better methods. Please tell me.

What would you [do, suggest, recommend, advise]?

That is a good [idea, suggestion, plan, proposal].

I like that. Let me think it over a little.

I like that. Let me work it out in my head.

Sounds like [a plan, an excellent idea]; it could work. (See "Grammar and Expressions.")

What is the [deadline for, time line on] that [job, project, work]?

When is the [job, project, work] due?

If you would like to talk about the way we approached that in (your country), I would like to share that.

There was a similar approach in (your country)—may I explain it?

You might be interested in how we did that in (your country)—may I explain it?

Culture Hint: *Time plays a very important role in business in the United States. Being on time to work and even for social engagements is expected. If you are going to be unavoidably late, you are expected to call. There are many idioms and proverbs in English concerning time and its importance. "Time is of the essence," "Time is money," "Time waits for no man," "No time to kill," "There is no time to lose," "Run out of time," "On time," "It's about time," and "Time is up" are examples of these.*

Grammar and Expressions

"Sounds like a plan." Instead of using the entire sentence "It sounds like a plan" or "This sounds like a plan," a shorter, idiomatic expression is often used, especially when referring to the five senses (sight, hearing, feeling, taste, and smell). For example, you may walk outside on a cold day in September and say, "Feels like winter." You may walk into your office at 9 A.M. on a workday and find it empty; you might say, "Looks like a weekend." If someone has been smoking, you might say, "Smells like a fire in here." If you like a dish in a restaurant, you might say, "Tastes like my mother's cooking."

Idioms and Other Vocabulary

Nevertheless: regardless of what happened before
Outside-the-box: out of the ordinary
Streamline: make something work better
Time is of the essence: time is very important

Part 1 Notes Section

Part 2

Small Talk

Chess Champion

We had an advanced English as a Second Language (ESL) student who had been a chess champion in his country and—until he became one here—needed to further his language skills for job interviews. This man was very **personable**; he was well-dressed, looked professional, and had an **engaging smile**. Our first meeting was similar to a job interview in that Boris introduced himself, handed me an impressive résumé, and told me about his job qualifications and his interest in chess. Then there was silence. I asked questions, similar to those a job interviewer might ask, and there continued to be silence. Boris understood the questions but spent so long considering his answers that I knew that the listener, even though patient, would become uncomfortable. The listener would then try to make himself or herself clearer, attempting everything to be able to communicate with Boris.

Boris's issue was that he considered every word he wanted to say to be a chess move. "If I say this, then what would a company job interviewer say?" Through many targeted exercises, Boris conquered his "fear of making a wrong move or saying a wrong word" and eventually was placed in an appropriate work situation. He continues to play chess and is able to switch from his "chess thinking" mode to a speaking-with-people mode.

Chapter 5

Interacting in a Small Group

Americans are not comfortable with silence; long periods of no talking and thinking silently present challenges. Many people, even those born and raised in the United States, are uncomfortable in any situation in which **small talk** is expected. You may be in a small group at work—around the watercooler, during a coffee break, at lunch, or waiting for a meeting to start—and chatting or making small talk.

Business entertaining is also part of American culture, so you may find yourself in these situations as well. Finding some **common** conversational **ground** may take a few tries. Therefore, **icebreakers** (often having to do with sports, current events, family life, and the weather) and humorous phrases are used to reduce nervousness. It is equally important to know what topics are **taboo**, such as inappropriate humor, sex, politics, religion, salaries, and personal financial issues.

Sometimes, smiling and being friendly and polite are all it takes to ease the tension. Always introduce yourself, if you haven't met before. Say your name twice, "Hi, I am Seema, Seema Patel." Ask the other person for his or her name if you don't know it. If you repeat the name of the other person after it has been said, you have a better chance of remembering it, "Nice to meet you, William." Listen carefully and stay focused; this will help you continue this conversation and prepare you for the next time you meet this person. Eye contact shows that you are interested and involved. So does body language; act as though you are comfortable and confident, even if you are not. However, if you really want a **leg up** in the small talk **arena**, the better informed you become on a wide variety of subjects, the more easily you will be able to handle **chitchat** or casual conversation. In addition to reading, watching, and listening to everything you can, practice small talk outside of work with everyone from neighbors to local merchants. **Open-ended questions** lead to more conversation and work better in encouraging small talk than yes and no questions.

Phrases About the Weather

Do you know the weather report for [tomorrow, the weekend, Sunday]?

The weather report predicts a lot of [rain, snow, wind, ice, hail, sun] this weekend.

What a [cold, unusually warm, snowy] winter this has been.

This has been a beautiful summer!

Do you think this rain will ever stop?

Is it supposed to rain this weekend?

Can you believe how hot it was last weekend?

I'd like to go to the beach tomorrow, but it is supposed to be [cloudy, windy, cold, rainy].

I have never seen so many [cold, hot, rainy, humid] days in a row.

Do you think there will be a break in the [heat, cold, snow, humidity]?

We need some [sun, rain, warm weather, cooler weather].

*Have you ever been in a [hurricane, **flash flood**, tornado, **blizzard**]?*

In my country it is now summer and about 85°F.

Phrases About Sports

Did you enjoy the [Super Bowl, World Series, All-Star Game]?

[Did you see, Are you going to watch, Are you going to go to] the game [tonight, this weekend, on Sunday]?

Do you play [golf, chess, badminton, tennis, soccer, basketball, hockey, baseball, softball, American football]?

Where can I go [swimming, skiing, boating, fishing, dancing, bowling, jogging] in this area?

I [play, like to play] [golf, chess, badminton, tennis, soccer, basketball, hockey, baseball, softball, American football].

I played [soccer, cricket, snooker, badminton, ice hockey, golf] in my country.

How about those [Mets, Yankees, Bears, Steelers, Devils]?

General Phrases

Think of questions to ask others in conjunction with giving information about yourself. Ask for someone else's opinions and share yours.

*Sometimes when I talk in a group, I get [nervous, **tongue-tied**, confused]. Does that happen to you?*

What do you think of . . . ?

Have you heard . . . ?

*What is your **take on** . . . ?*

What do you do [in your free time, in your leisure time, on weekends, on vacations]?

Do you have kids? How old are they?

*Do you go to movies? What type of films do you like? I like [mysteries, romance, horror, **tear-jerkers**, comedies, musicals].*

*Are you in a [**reading group, book club**]?*

Can you recommend a good [mystery biography, novel]?

*Have you tried **Sudoku**?*

*I'm addicted to **Sudoku** [the crossword puzzle, Trivial Pursuit, Scrabble, board games].*

Do you live in the city? There is so much going on there.

I went to a street fair last weekend. Have you ever been to one around here?

The interactive children's museum is great.

I never learned to play a musical instrument. I always wanted to play the [piano, guitar, violin, oboe, viola]. Do you play an instrument?

*Is there a **Toastmasters** group in the company?*

*It's almost five o'clock, and I can't wait to [**call it a day, get a move on**].*

*It's a weekend, **TGIF**.*

*This week seems so long, but it's only Monday afternoon! I can't wait until **hump day.***

*I can even catch the **happy hour** at the local restaurant.*

*I haven't seen you for a couple of days. Have you been [on vacation, out of town, on a business trip, **under the weather**]?*

*I went to my first annual meeting yesterday, and I learned a lot. I had the opportunity to [participate, **chime in**, **catch up**, be heard].*

Ending a Casual Conversation

Well, [my break is over, it's getting late, the lunch hour went quickly, I have to get back to my desk].

I am [sorry, afraid] I have to [go, leave, get back].

I'm sorry—I have to run to a meeting.

I'm sorry—I have to go, but let's talk more this afternoon.

Excuse me—I have to join a conference call.

It was [nice, good, interesting, a pleasure] talking to you.

I enjoyed [talking to, meeting, chatting with] you.

See you [later, after the meeting, at the end of the conference].

[I am sure, I hope, I know] we will see each other again.

I see my [boss, colleague, client, customer, friend] [over there, across the room]. Please excuse me.

*I have another meeting. Can we [**wrap up** this discussion, finish later, meet tomorrow]?*

Culture Hints: *When searching for words, use pauses (short moments of silence) to leave time to think instead of saying "um," "uh," "er," or "you know." However, don't pause too long. Americans are not comfortable with silence and may not be patient. They might jump in and interrupt you before you continue your thought. There is another technique for giving yourself more time to think. Have a bottle of water **handy** and when you need a little extra time, take a **sip** before continuing to speak.*

Also, remember that what you are saying in these casual conversations doesn't have to be grammatically perfect, just understood.

Phrases to Say Before Pausing

Please give me a moment.

I need a minute to think of a word.

May I have a second or two to think?

I'd like to continue, please.

Culture Hint: *Toastmasters is an international organization devoted to improving public speaking. There are groups in many companies as well as public groups that meet in libraries and other public places. A Toastmasters group is often a good place to build presentation skills and to cure jittery nerves. These groups are reasonably priced and certainly worth an initial meeting or two to at least observe the proceedings.*

Idioms and Other Vocabulary

Arena: area around a subject, e.g., "the small talk arena"

Blizzard: a really bad snowstorm with high winds

Call it a day: stop working for the day

Catch up: to gain information or knowledge in order to get to the level of others

Chime in: add to a conversation

Chitchat: talk about unimportant subjects

Common ground: shared interests

Engaging smile: a smile that brings positive attention

Flash flood: dangerously large amount of water caused by rapid rainfall

Get a move on: hurry up

Handy: near and easy to reach

Happy hour: time when bars serve alcoholic beverages during early evening hours at discount prices

Hump day: Wednesday—the middle day of the workweek for most people (Once you pass hump day, the week is almost over.)

Icebreakers: things said to make initial conversations more at ease

Leg up: a head start

Open-ended questions: questions without definite answers, not yes or no questions

Personable: attractive

Reading group or book club: a group in which all the participants read the same book or author and then meet to discuss the book or books by the author

Sip: a small amount of a drink

Small talk: talk about unimportant subjects

Sudoku: a crossword-type puzzle with numbers instead of letters and words

Taboo: something to be avoided

Take on: opinion of

Tear-jerker: a sad movie, story, or book

TGIF: acronym for Thank God It's Friday!

Toastmasters: an international public-speaking group. "Toast" comes from the custom of raising a glass to say nice things about a person, people, or groups. Toasts are usually made on special occasions (weddings, anniversaries, job promotions, retirements, to name a few). A "master" is someone who excels at something. Toastmasters is devoted to helping people improve their public speaking skills.

Tongue-tied: not able to speak easily out of nervousness or embarrassment

Under the weather: not feeling well, feeling sick

Wrap up: to end, to finish, to close

Chapter 6

Giving and Accepting Compliments

A compliment is a positive remark of praise, admiration, or approval. Everyone values honest acknowledgment of a job done well or an attractive object or a fine quality. Giving a compliment is more often said as "paying a compliment." People from the United States tend to pay compliments more easily and more often than people from other countries. There is, however, a fine line between never paying a compliment and over-complimenting. You don't want to compliment everyone on everything; excessive complimenting to a person is **flattery** or over-praise. The related word, ***flattered***, can be used in a positive way as well, "Your report was so good that the boss wants to use it at the regional meeting." "Well, I am really flattered [honored]."

Another related expression is "fishing for compliments," or attempting to manipulate someone into saying something nice about you. For example, a colleague may say, "This assignment is beyond me; my English isn't good enough for me to attend such a large meeting and to talk to so many people in English." The colleague may be waiting for you to say, "Of course you can. Your English is improving every day, there will be other foreign nationals there, and the **CEO** wants you to represent the company. He chose you."

Other related phrases are "left-handed compliment" or "back-handed compliment." These expressions refer to an insult disguised as a compliment, and they often border on **sarcasm**. A compliment is "That's a beautiful coat"; flattery is "That's a beautiful coat, your scarf is also lovely, and I've never seen such magnificent boots." A left-handed compliment would be "That coat is beautiful; it was a very popular style ten years ago."

Phrases Used to Compliment

That was an excellent presentation.

I'd like to compliment you on your [report, presentation, performance, idea].

Your report was [impressive, very informative, exceptional, wonderful].

*You are a **dynamic** presenter!*

*I was impressed with your [report, presentation, performance]. It was [clear, complete, **on target**, accurate].*

*Your **PowerPoint** presentation was detailed and informative.*

I wish I could [write, present, speak] that well.

You speak so easily and clearly at meetings.

Your ideas for the project are [useful, refreshing, thought-provoking].

Your feedback was helpful.

That was a valuable point at the meeting today. Thank you for sharing it.

*I appreciate that you are always willing to [**cover for** coworkers, **cover** the phones, come in early, change shifts with me].*

Thank you for [covering for coworkers, covering my phones, coming in early, changing shifts with me].

Your English is really improving. Every time you [make a presentation, submit a report, conduct a meeting] you sound more professional.

Is that your family in the picture on your desk? What a beautiful family.

I like what you did with your office.

I loved the brownies you made for the office; they were delicious.

It is often difficult to respond to a compliment. Sometimes we feel embarrassed or not worthy of praise. People may say, "Oh, it was nothing," when in fact it took a lot of work. It is better to respond honestly with a simple "Thank you."

Phrases Used to Accept Compliments

Thank you.

Thanks.

Thank you, it is nice of you to say so.

Thanks for saying so.

Thank you, I really worked hard on this report.

Thanks, I really appreciate [that, your comments, your interest, your input, your feedback].

I'm glad you [liked, enjoyed, learned from] the [report, presentation, meeting].

I'm really working on my [English, presentation skills, writing skills, pronunciation skills]. Thank you for noticing.

I appreciate your comments.

I'm glad you liked the brownies. I made them from scratch.

I am happy you enjoyed my baking. It is my mother's recipe.

Saying "thank you" is more polite and formal than "thanks." Therefore, "thank you" is used in more formal situations such as job interviews, meetings, speaking with upper management, and superiors.

Culture Hints: When complimenting people in the United States on a personal item, such as clothing, a car, or a home, it is impolite to ask how much it cost. You may ask where they bought the item or how they found it. On a professional level, however, if your job involves budgeting or monitoring expenses; you not only have the right, but the duty to know what company expenditures are.

People from cultures in which modesty and humility are important and being part of "the group" is a core value, and individuality is not, will often have great difficulty accepting compliments. In some countries people compliment very little, once a week or less frequently. In the United States we compliment often, sometimes many times a day.

The word **complement** is often confused with the word **compliment** that we have been discussing. **Complement** means "to complete the whole." For example, when you do part of a presentation, your colleague may do another part to complement yours and make the presentation complete.

37

Idioms and Other Vocabulary

CEO: Chief Executive Officer
Cover: take care of
Cover for: take over for; do the work of
Dynamic: full of energy
Flattered: pleased with praise
Flattery: excessive praise
On target: to the point
PowerPoint: a popular software program that enables the user to present ideas in a series of slides
Sarcasm: saying the opposite of what one means in order to make a joke that is sometimes unkind. For example, "I have been with the company for two wonderful years; two out of five aren't bad."

Chapter 7

Giving, Accepting, and Refusing Invitations

In the United States, formal events (weddings, anniversaries, bridal or baby showers, and other **rites of passage**) and, sometimes, less formal events (luncheons, dinner parties, office parties, and birthday parties) use printed or written invitations to invite people to attend. Today, many people send informal invitations as e-mail attachments or even within the e-mail itself.

Invitations are addressed to—and only to—the people the host or hostess wants to attend the event. An invitation may be addressed to you and your spouse or partner (if a person inviting you knows the other person or it may be addressed to you and a guest). If an invitation is not addressed to your family or your children, don't assume they are invited; they are not.

"R.S.V.P." with a date is printed or written on most invitations. The initials R.S.V.P. are for the French *répondez s'il vous plait*, which means "respond if you please." This is a polite way to say you must answer. The date printed near the R.S.V.P. is the date by which you must reply. Sometimes a small return card with a stamped, self-addressed return envelope is enclosed in the invitation. This must be mailed back on time. The host or hostess needs a **headcount** to inform caterers about food quantities and to arrange seating. A formal invitation may also have the phrase "Black Tie" or "Black Tie Optional." Black tie indicates formal attire—a **tux** for a man and dressy attire for a woman.

A reply card is a small card to be returned to the host(s) by a certain date. On this card you indicate whether or not you will attend and, often, your menu preference (meat, chicken, fish, or vegetarian). A stamped, self-addressed envelope is usually enclosed. This makes it convenient to reply and to reply on time. Sometimes there is no reply card, only a phone number to call with an answer.

A less formal invitation may be given by mail, e-mail, or telephone. Sometimes an invitation has "Regrets Only" with a telephone number. This means, call only if you are unable to attend, otherwise the host or hostess assumes you will be there. Also, a party may be a surprise party. In this case, the hosts do not want the guest of honor to know about it because they want to surprise the guest. It is very important not to **let the cat out of the bag** and also to be sure to be on time so you don't spoil the surprise.

Casual or last-minute invitations are often given by e-mail or telephone or in person. All invitations must be answered, and, if you are unable to attend, it is impolite not to respond at all or to just say no. Offer a reason why you can't attend the event or say something to **buy time** to think further.

In the United States, some people close conversations with phrases that sound like invitations, but really are not. These expressions include:

Stop over sometime.

Let's get together sometime.

We really should meet again soon.

Please stop by, if you are in the neighborhood.

Drop in when you can.

Don't be a stranger.

Let's do lunch.

Are you free sometime?

When an expression like, "Don't be a stranger" is followed by "Give me a call sometime" or "Let's get together soon," the speaker does want to get together with you. This is a first step toward a real invitation. People can be busy and **caught up** with family and other commitments. As much as they want to and plan to make a **firm date**, they may not get to it as quickly as they would like to.

However, actual invitations are definite. While the person who offers **offhand** invitations like "stop over sometime" may be sincere, most people consider it rude just to **drop in** without actually being invited or at least calling to check if the time is convenient.

An invitation for a meal may be to someone's home. Sometimes friends have a **potluck dinner**—everyone brings a dish to contribute to the meal. When you go to someone's home, whether or not you are bringing part of the dinner, you could bring some small gift, like a bottle of wine, a box of candy, or flowers. An especially **nice touch** is to bring a souvenir from your native country.

Other dinner invitations are to be someone's guest at a restaurant or just to join someone for dinner **Dutch treat**. On occasion, someone may say, "It's on me," which means the person inviting you intends to pay the bill. You may also be invited to join someone at a concert or sporting event as a guest. Some invitations are **spur of the moment** such as getting together for coffee.

Phrases Used to Give Invitations

Let's have lunch together. I'd like to discuss the [meeting, presentation]; I didn't understand it all.

Can you join me in the cafeteria for [coffee, lunch]?

When are you free for lunch this week?

Let's plan on having lunch this week. When is good for you?

Do you have time for a long lunch?

Do you want to try that new restaurant in the building for lunch?

Would you like to take a coffee break this afternoon to discuss [the meeting, the project, the report, my latest work]?

Would you like to go out for a drink tomorrow night after work?

Do you play [tennis, golf, basketball, bridge, chess, cards]? I'd like to [play, have a game, start a group] after work.

We're having a [dinner party, get-together, gathering, barbeque, wine and cheese party] this Saturday evening. Would you like to join us?

When inviting someone, start by telling them the event, the day, and time. Do not start by saying, "Are you free Saturday evening?" Being specific about your plan and the activity gives the other person a chance to decide on whether or not he or she wants to attend the event. Otherwise, the person invited may accept the invitation not knowing that the event is not **to his or her taste**. In that case, that person could be in the **awkward** situation of having to figure out how to get out of the **engagement**.

[I, My wife and I, My husband and I, My partner and I, My family and I] would like [you, you and your wife, you and your husband, you and your partner, you and your family] to join us for [brunch, lunch, dinner, a small gathering, a picnic, a wine and cheese party].

*We would like to invite [you, you and your wife, you and your husband, you and your partner, you and your family] to a **get-together** at our home next Sunday. Are you free?*

*There is a great [Indian, French, Hungarian, new] restaurant in town. Would you like to try it for lunch one day next week? We'll **go Dutch**.*

Phrases Used to Accept Invitations

Thank you, I'd really like to join you.

That would be wonderful. Yes.

Yes, I can, and tomorrow is fine.

I'd love to.

I'm looking forward to it.

I'd like to [be there, join you, attend].

Yes. Thanks for [asking me, thinking of me, including me].

Yes, I can take a little longer for lunch with you.

Phrases Used to Refuse Invitations

I'm sorry, I have a previous engagement.

*I'm sorry, I [am busy, am **tied up**, have another appointment].*

*I'm sorry—I'm **booked** all week with a conference.*

Sorry, I can't make it. How about another time?

I can't tomorrow, but I can another day.

I'm sorry, I can't go tomorrow. Would next week work for you instead?

*I would love to join you next time. I won't be **able to make it** [tomorrow, next week, then].*

That would be wonderful, but I'm out of town. How about . . . ?

Please ask me again.

*How about a **rain check**?*

Sorry, I can't make it. Thank you for inviting me. (If you don't want another invitation don't ask for a rain check.)

Phrases Used to Clarify Invitations

*Is this **on the company**?*

*Does the company **cover** this expense?*

May I charge this to my expense account?

Is there parking?

May I [bring, make, bake, cook] something?

*Is this a **potluck dinner**?*

I make a great apple pie. Would you like me to bring one?

I noticed that this barbeque is on Sunday. Are there going to be kids there?

Are family members invited?

*What is the **dress code** for this party?*

What do [people, women, men] usually wear to this kind of event?

How do [people, women, men] usually dress for this?

Are work clothes okay for this event?

Will it be okay if I'm fifteen minutes late?

Phrases Used to Buy Time Before Responding to Invitations

Let me check [with my wife, with my husband, with my partner, my calendar, my schedule].

I'll let you know [later, tomorrow, Monday].

I may [be working, be away, have a previous engagement]. Let me get back to you as soon as I check.

I'm sorry, I can't confirm my schedule until the conference is over. As soon as I know, I will tell you.

I'd love to go, but let me check my calendar first to be sure I don't have a(n) [conflict, obligation].

I'm not sure when my meeting will end; can I [call, text, e-mail] you when I'm done?

Thank you for thinking of me, but I may have to go out of town. Let me check and get back to you.

Let me be sure I can get a babysitter and I will let you know. Thank you.

Culture Hints: In many countries there are no "false" invitations. When people ask you to their homes they always mean it. Don't take it literally when someone in the United States says, "Drop by any time." Call first.

There are many occasions that are celebrated in the United States. Don't feel pressured to accept every social invitation you may receive. However, it is important to accept as many business-related invitations as possible.

Americans often mix socializing with business. As a culture, we spend so much time working with colleagues, who then become friends, that it is a natural extension to socialize with work acquaintances. Additionally, Americans take less vacation time than people in most other countries. This increases their time at work and time spent with colleagues.

*It is important when you promise to get back to a host after checking your availability, that you do get back with an answer in time for the host to plan. Americans are often busy with family obligations such as their children's sporting events and games. Your colleagues may also be visiting relatives or friends who live in another state. They may be entertaining these relatives or friends when they are here. Your American colleagues may want to approach you with an invitation but be booked way in advance for these family and friends events. It is not polite to invite yourself to someone's home, but you can make yourself **invitable**.*

Idioms and Other Vocabulary

Able to make it: able to attend
Awkward: makes someone feel uncomfortable
Booked: time is taken up with appointments
Buy time: to delay making a decision
Caught up: involved in
Cover: pay for
Dress code: rules about what to wear in a situation or to an event

Drop in: visit without notice, without making arrangements

Dutch treat: sharing the cost of a meal; each person paying for his or her own food; also known as **going Dutch**

Engagement: appointment

Firm date: set dates or appointments

Get-together: casual social gathering

Headcount: a count of how many people will attend

Invitable: friendly, smiling, making small talk, approachable

Let the cat out of the bag: to reveal a secret

Nice touch: a nice gesture, a nice thing to do

Offhand: casual, informal

On the company: the company pays for this, picks up the expense

Potluck dinner: everyone invited brings something to eat

Rain check: the possibility to do something at another time (From baseball, this means you may go back another time for free if the game is rained out.)

Rites of passage: important life events, life changing events, also called *milestones*

Spur of the moment: without planning ahead of time ("on the" or "at the" spur of the moment)

Tied up: busy, occupied

To his or her taste: to his or her liking

Tux: short for *tuxedo*

Part 2 Notes Section

Part 3

Using the Telephone

"Medicine"

When Sonia, a wonderful Peruvian nanny, spoke to my grandson Leo on the telephone, he had been home from day camp for several days with a cold. Sonia asked Leo, who was three-and-a-half years old at the time, "Are you going to camp today?" Leo answered, "Yes, because I have medicine." Sonia said, "What? Leo, I don't understand you." Leo said again, "Medicine." Sonia repeated, "I don't understand." Leo came back with, "Medicine, a-e-o-p-q-6-7, medicine." He couldn't spell yet, but he knew that people spelled for clarification, especially over the telephone.

Chapter 8

Speak Up and Speak Out

Speaking over the telephone has gotten more and more confusing—even for people who are fluent in English. Very often you are listening to and speaking to a machine—not a live person. Also there are many **prompts** to press to reach other machines and many minutes to wait before you can even try to understand someone and be understood by a real person. Therefore, you may be sure that even many people fluent in English are often confused. But you can master the telephone just as well as anyone else can.

If or when you do get to speak to an actual person, telephone talk is more difficult than speaking face-to-face because you cannot see facial expressions or body language. The person on the other end of the line cannot see your face or gestures, either. In addition, surrounding noises, on your side or on the other end, may interfere with listening and speaking.

Do not let any of this stop you from using the telephone! You need a lot of practice to feel comfortable, and you actually can get a lot of practice listening and becoming more comfortable with telephone skills before ever speaking with a live person over the phone.

Remember that listening is different from hearing. Hearing is passive. When your auditory sensors work, you are able to hear. Listening is active. Listening occurs when you choose to listen, focus on what is being said, understand what is being said, and are able to react.

Telephone Listening Practice

Through practice, you can become more comfortable using the telephone. Start by practicing your listening. First, call numbers that have recorded messages such as:

- **Movie phone lines.** These are often difficult to understand because people with no specific telephone presentation training are speaking rapidly on the recordings. Listen to the messages several times, and write down what you hear. For example, you may write, "Roxy Theater *Jurassic Park* 12 noon 3 P.M. 6 P.M." You may then check spelling and information in the newspaper or online.
- **Businesses.** Those that are closed for the weekend, evenings, or holidays have recorded messages. Again, listen to as many messages as you want. You will start to notice some messages are clear and professional and others are more difficult to comprehend.

Additional listening practice may include:

- **Telemarketers.** When they call, listen first and try to understand, and then you may say, "I am not interested."
- **Friends.** Ask them to call you so you can practice having telephone conversations or ask them to leave messages on your voice mail for your listening practice.

For even more practice, listen every chance you get to the radio, music on tapes or CDs, **books on tape, audio books on CD,** and live speech. Also, watch movies, news, **situation comedies**, **soap operas**,

51

cooking shows, educational programs, and other programs on TV and DVD.

Put a smile in your voice even when you speak over the telephone. Believe it or not, you sound better over the phone when you are **upbeat** and have a smile on your face. It's a good trick to put a mirror next to your phone on your desk to remind you to check your smile before you make a call or answer one. Another way to put a smile on your face is to put a picture that makes you happy next to the phone and look at it before you pick up the receiver to answer or make a telephone call. An important rule: don't eat, drink, or chew on anything while speaking on the phone. You would be surprised how obvious it is to the person on the other end of the line. Also, don't **multitask** while speaking on the telephone. Pay full attention to the call; it will **pay off**.

It is **crucial** to pay attention to your voice, since that is all the person on the other end has from which to get an impression of you. Don't put your hand in front of your face or mouth while speaking and never **mumble**. Remember to project your voice and speak clearly and slowly. Show interest and enthusiasm.

Whether answering a call or making one, it is important to have paper and pen or pencil **handy** to **jot down** information. Even with much business being conducted by e-mail **nowadays**, it is still important to be able to communicate effectively on the telephone. Write important questions you want to ask or have answered before you pick up the receiver. Write down key words or information as you listen.

Basically there are three sections to a call: an opening, a body or the purpose of the call, and the closing.

Initiating a Phone Call

For business calls, make sure you ask for the person you intend to reach. You should know the name and title and be certain how to pronounce both correctly.

Hello, this is (your name) [with, from, of] (your company).

I would like to speak to (name of the person or the department you are calling).

May I speak with (name of the person or the department you are calling)?

Is this a good time to speak briefly about . . . ?

When would be a better time to call about . . . ?

What is the best time to call about . . . ?

Personal phone calls or internal phone calls may start more informally.

Hi, this is (your first name).

Do you have time to talk for a few minutes?

Have you got a minute?

Are you busy?

Can we talk now?

Is this a good time to talk?

Phrases to Move Along a Phone Call

Clearly and precisely state your purpose for calling. Remember focus and simplicity. Be certain you understand everything about the call. Don't pretend to understand, don't **fake it**. Slow down. Speak more slowly than when speaking your native language. If you slow down your pace, often the person on the other end will follow and slow down as well.

I won't take up too much of your time, I just need to ask you about . . .

I appreciate your time. I hope that this will only take five minutes.

*I just wanted to **touch base** with you for five minutes about . . .*

Is this an area you handle?

Could you tell me the person I should speak with instead?

Phrases to Get Clarification

Please speak a little slower because I want to take notes.

Let me repeat what you said to be sure I have it correctly.

Pardon me for interrupting, but did you say . . . ?

Did you mean . . . ?

Are you saying that . . . ?

Would you mind repeating that?

I didn't [get that, understand that]. Please [spell, repeat] that.

To be sure I understand . . . (repeat what you have heard).

I see, so . . . (repeat what you have heard)

***Bear with me**, I just want to write that down.*

Could you clarify what you just said?

Excuse me, I don't [follow, get, understand] what you are saying.

Please say that [again, more slowly, louder].

Phrases to Close a Phone Call

Before ending a phone call, confirm the next step for you and the other person to take. Often, after a phone call ends and both parties hang up, the caller doesn't know what the next step is.

I will get back to you.

We will speak about this again.

Let me clear it with my [boss, department, team, committee].

I will look up the [answer, schedule, fax] and get back to you.

Would you prefer that I e-mail it to you?

It was nice to hear from you again.

Thanks for [calling, returning my call, getting back to me].

Thank you for [bringing this to my attention, pointing this out]. I will change it.

Thank you for your time. I appreciate the explanation.

Thank you for going over this with me. I understand now.

I will follow up this conversation with an e-mail that summarizes our decisions.

I will tell my boss what we discussed and get back to you at the end of the week.

Can you let me know by [the end of the day, Friday, the first]?

I have to discuss this with my colleagues before I can decide, but I will let you know by [date, time].

I will send an e-mail with the report attached.

Culture Hint: *Telemarketers are people who sell products or services or ask for contributions over the telephone. These calls have expanded to recorded* **sales pitches.** *Some calls are legitimate, and others may be* **scams** *or* **frauds.** *There is a National Do Not Call Registry where you may list your telephone number and request not to be called by telemarketers.*

Phrases to Respond to Telemarketing Phone Calls

Thank you, but I am not interested.

I never [buy, purchase, contribute] over the telephone.

No, I am not interested.

No, thank you.

No.

Idioms and Other Vocabulary

Bear with me: give me additional time, be patient with me
Books on tape/audio books on CD: books recorded on tape or CD
Crucial: critical, everything else relies on it
Fake it: pretend
Frauds: deceptions used to obtain something illegally
Handy: useful; simple to use
Jot down: write notes quickly
Multitask: do several things at the same time
Mumble: speak quietly and unclearly
Nowadays: at the present

Pay off: it will be worth it

Prompts: recorded instructions over the telephone

Sales pitches: techniques for convincing people to buy products or services

Scams: fraudulent schemes to get money

Situation comedies: TV comedy series about people whose lives include situations that are easy to relate to (see themselves in) and laugh at when other people are in them (often called *sitcoms*, e.g., *Seinfeld* and *30 Rock*)

Soap operas: continuing TV stories about the same group of people with tragic plots similar to operas; originate from programs that advertised soap

Touch base: connect with someone for a short time

Upbeat: optimistic

Chapter 9

Your Voice Mail

Create your own voice mail message, correct it, and practice it. Do not use a **canned message**. Record the message in your own voice, even if you have an accent. Play it back, listen to it, and re-record the message until you are satisfied. Remember, smile while recording and speak slowly. Practice your message until you are able to say it without reading it. To check intelligibility, play your message for an associate or friend whose first language is English.

Phrases for Recording a Message

This is (your name) (your department/company).

I am not available to answer your call right now.

I am [at a meeting, away from my desk, on another call].

I am [on vacation, at a conference, on extended leave].

Please leave a brief message including your name, telephone number, and the best time to [call you back, reach you, get in touch with you, talk, speak].

I will call you [this afternoon, tomorrow morning, Monday, as soon as possible].

If you need to speak to someone immediately, [you may press zero for the operator, call my secretary at ext. 234].

I am on vacation until _____, but I will be checking [phone messages, e-mail, faxes].

I will be on vacation from _____ to _____ without access to voice mail or e-mail. Please contact _____.

I will be out of the office from _____ to _____ with limited access to voice mail and e-mail.

If you wish to send me an e-mail, the address is _____.

If you wish to send a fax, the number is _____.

Culture Hint: Mostly everyone in the United States has voice mail on office telephones, home phones, and cell phones. Sometimes people put their cell phone numbers on their business cards, especially if they are often out of the office.

Idioms and Other Vocabulary

Canned message: prerecorded telephone message to put on your voice mail

Limited access: often, when people are out of their offices for several days, they cannot return voice-mail or e-mail messages. By saying that they have limited access, they are letting others know that they may not be able to listen to or read messages or respond to them. These messages often will refer the caller or sender to someone else who can provide immediate assistance.

Chapter 10

Leaving Messages

When making a phone call, have a message ready (written out, practiced, and ready to say) in case the person you have called isn't in and you have to leave a message on that person's voice mail. Don't **hesitate** to leave a message on an answering machine. Don't leave a **vague** message. Give specific information. Be **concise**; make the message short and to the point. Include the important information, containing your name and telephone number—twice, at the beginning and at the end of the message so that people have a chance to process the information. Speak slowly and speak up; don't let your voice drop before you finish your message.

When leaving a telephone number, say each number separately: "nine-seven-three," *not* "nine seventy-three." Always repeat phone numbers. If your phone number includes the number 0, you can say either "O" or "zero." The only time not to pronounce each number separately is if the number ends in hundreds (800) or thousands (8000) (e.g., 555-345-0800, or 555-345-8000). Pause before and after numbers, names, and other important words.

Some letters sound exactly like other letters when pronounced. It is a good idea to use an example of the letters to make them clear to the listener. As you spell your name over the telephone, either to a person or a machine, clarify each letter with simple words that you know you pronounce well, for example, *a* as in *apple* (not *aunt*, which is pronounced differently in different parts of the United States).

A as in *apple*
B as in *blue*
C as in *Charles*
D as in *David*
E as in *easy*
F as in *Frank*
G as in *green*
H as in *Henry*
I as in *ice*
J as in *John*
K as in *king*
L as in *Larry*
M as in *Mary*
N as in *Nancy*
O as in *orange*
P as in *Peter*
Q as in *queen*
R as in *red*
S as in *Sam*
T as in *Tom*
U as in *umbrella*
V as in *Victor*
W as in *Walter*
X as in *x-ray*
Y as in *yellow*
Z as in *zebra*

Speak loudly and articulate to ensure that the recipient can understand the information you provide, since he or she cannot ask you for clarification. Follow this K.I.S.S. rule—**K**eep **I**t **S**imple and **S**mile.

Phrases for Leaving Messages

This is (first name, last name) with (your company).

I'm calling about _____ .

I'm calling in regard to _____ .

I'm returning your call from this morning.

Again, this is (first name, last name), and my telephone number is _____ .

Please call me at _____ . I'm available from 9 A.M. to 6 P.M.

Phrases to Use When Taking Messages for Others

Write down key information, including the name of the caller, the time and date of the phone call, the caller's telephone number, and the best time for the caller to be reached. Also include the **nature of the phone call** if **relevant**. Even if the caller claims that the person he or she is leaving the message for has the phone number, politely ask the caller for the phone number anyway so it can be included in the message.

May I have your name and telephone number, please?

When may [he, she] return your phone call?

Where can you be reached?

May I tell [him, her] what your phone call is in reference to?

Would you mind repeating that?

Would you mind spelling your name for me, please?

[Would you, Could you] hold a moment while I write that down?

Let me repeat your message and telephone number back to you.

Is that correct?

Culture Hint: *If you have listened to voice mails, you know how difficult they are to understand even when people speak slowly and clearly. The technology may not be perfect. Be direct and only leave the necessary information. Save all the details for the actual telephone call. Remember to write your message down in case the person you are trying to reach isn't available and you have to leave a message.*

Idioms and Other Vocabulary

Concise: short, no unnecessary words
Hesitate: pause
Nature of the phone call: subject of the call
Relevant: having to do with
Vague: not clear

Chapter 11

Speaking with Someone Who Is Difficult to Understand

If someone is speaking quickly, speak slowly and the person on the other end of the line will most likely keep pace by slowing down. When you have trouble understanding someone and part of the problem is that person is speaking very rapidly, try this pacing technique. Ask the person to spell the particular word or name. The caller may initially spell as quickly as he or she speaks. Interrupting this spelling with your own repetition—and at a slower pace—will slow the other person down.

> **You:** Please spell your last name; I didn't understand it.
> **Other Person (rapidly):** *S-m-i-t-h*
> **You:** Again, please. Could you spell more slowly?
> **Other Person:** *S*
> **You:** *S*
> **Other Person:** *M*
> **You:** *M*

Continue repeating every letter you hear before the other person has a chance to say the next letter. This will confirm that you heard the correct letter, and it will slow down the process. Spell the entire name along with the other person, and at the end say the name, in this case "Smith."

Don't fake understanding. It might come back to **haunt you**. Do not be afraid to ask questions. There are no dumb questions! It is better to ask a question twice than to act on the wrong information. Moreover, it is better to ask for clarification as soon as possible by using some of the following expressions, or by substituting your own specific questions or requests.

Phrases to Ask for Clarification

I couldn't follow what you said.

I am not sure I follow you.

*Excuse me, but I don't know what you mean. Could you please **rephrase** that?*

Please say that again.

Would you mind repeating that again?

Let me be sure I've got your information . . . (repeat it)

Did you say m *as in* Mary?

Is that central time or eastern time?

Is that your local time or our local time?

Did I understand you to say [this afternoon, at 4:00 P.M., in conference room C]?

Please speak more slowly.

Whom do you want?

What do you want?

Where are we meeting?

When is the meeting?

What time is the meeting?

What should I bring to this meeting?

Pardon me, you did say [noon, cafeteria, after work], didn't you?

I didn't catch that. Please repeat it.

How do you pronounce your name? I really want to say it correctly. (Repeat the information back to the caller and have him or her agree or correct it.)

Culture Hint: A lot of business is conducted over the telephone in the United States. Even Americans spell frequently on the phone. They also ask for clarification often. It isn't just because you, or the person to whom you are speaking, has an accent that spelling and repetition are used as telephone clarification tools.

Idioms and Other Vocabulary

Didn't catch that: I didn't hear/understand that
Haunt you: cause problems
Rephrase: say it in other words

Chapter 12

Speaking with Someone Who Has Difficulty Understanding You

When talking to someone who is having a hard time understanding you, speak slowly, more slowly than you speak in your native language. You can also ask the person to repeat what you said to make sure he or she did understand.

Phrases to Use When Someone Has Trouble Understanding You

Sometimes my accent is difficult to understand. Please let me know that you understood what I said.

Please repeat what you heard me say, so that I know I have been clear.

Yes, that is m as in Mary, a as in apple . . .

Thank you for your patience.

I might have spoken too quickly; let me repeat what I said.

Please tell me if I'm not being clear.

Perhaps I can rephrase that.

Are you sure you understood what I said?

Are you certain you understand that?

Let me repeat that.

Let me say that again.

I will say that in another way.

Let me say that in other words.

Please let me spell that.

*I would like to **rephrase** that.*

May I clarify that?

Let me make sure I said that correctly.

What do you understand about . . . ?

Did you get that?

***Feel free** to interrupt me [with questions, if you don't understand me, if you want me to repeat or spell something].*

Ask the person on the other end of the line to repeat the information back to you to be sure he or she understood it correctly.

Culture Hint: After a phone call with important information, it is a good idea to follow up with an e-mail to confirm what was said in the call. Names and numbers are especially significant details to focus on in your e-mail.

Idioms and Other Vocabulary

Feel free: go ahead, don't worry about it
Rephrase: say it in other words

Part 3 Notes Section

Part 4

Presenting Yourself

"A White Joke"

Customized Language Skills Training (CLST) offered a small group class for presentation skills and three people enrolled. The assignment was to plan, work on, and give a presentation to a small audience.

The first participant, Ricardo, wanted to tell a joke to introduce his presentation. The other two trainees, Kim and Olga, questioned this method. Olga was bad at telling **jokes** and, therefore, nervous about doing so. Kim thought maybe the joke would be inappropriate. Ricardo said, "No, it's a white joke." I had never heard that expression before and found out that day that it meant a "clean joke" to this South American man as opposed to a **dirty, off-color**, or **blue joke.**

Olga's presentation included a portion on telling a **lie**. Since she was using the expression several times, she wanted to know other words for a lie. Ricardo suggested "white lie," "fib," and "untruth." Kim shouted out, "Is bullshit a lie?" The room became silent and all three looked at me. I said, "Yes, actually it is, but that isn't a 'white' word so don't use it at work." We all laughed and moved on.

Chapter 13

Before You Present

When do you need presentation skills? Any time you must speak to others and want to **make a good impression**.

What to say really depends on the situation. You may simply be walking down the hallway and meet the **CEO** of the company or anyone else. You may be in a small group of coworkers or at an outside meeting. You may be a participant in a small discussion group, called upon to present an idea to your department, or you may be part of a panel on a particular subject. Also, you might be asked to present in your area of expertise to a larger group. Other situations include talking with customers, clients, guests, or patients.

Of course, if you are only communicating for a few minutes you won't need many of these presentation suggestions. It **won't hurt**, however, to **skim** them and select what you can use now and refer to the list as you need more help.

In the United States, people often use name tags, badges, or **tent cards** to identify participants at meetings, presentations, or **networking events**. These do not replace trying to remember names in a smaller group. They help, however, if you forget a name or are part of a larger group, in which there are many names to remember. Saying others' names correctly is important and not always easy. **Jump into**

it. When someone introduces himself or herself, repeat the name out loud in context: "Nice to meet you, Clarence." If you have trouble **pronouncing** the name, ask the person to help you. People are usually **flattered** that you care enough to say their names correctly. Similarly, when saying your name, say it slowly, clearly, and twice: "Hello, I am Natalie, Natalie Gast." If you are with coworkers who probably know your name, you can still **jog** their **memories** or reinforce **pronunciation** by saying your name.

Phrases to Get Information About an Assignment—Content

You need to get as much information about your presentation parameters as possible. Ask as many questions as you need as often as you need to feel comfortable.

How long do you want me to speak?

How long is the presentation?

How much time is allotted for my part?

Will others be speaking as well?

Will there be a panel?

Who are the other presenters?

Who will make the introductory remarks?

*Will this be a **virtual presentation**?*

Do you want me to speak on a particular topic?

Do you want me to choose my own topic?

Do you want me to speak about my area of expertise?

Do you want me to speak about my country?

Do questions and answers follow the presentation or come during the presentation?

I would like to have a ten-minute question-and-answer session.

*Should I use [visuals, **PowerPoint**, a flip chart, a **white board**, handouts]?*

How many people are expected to be in the audience?

Shall I prepare an agenda?

Should I send out an agenda before the presentation?

*Do you have someone who can **coach** me on my presentation?*

Do you have time to listen to my presentation before I give it?

I would feel more comfortable if we rehearsed the presentation beforehand.

Phrases to Get Information About an Assignment—Materials

*I need [a projector, a laptop, a **white board**, a **flip chart**, an electrical outlet].*

Will there be a [microphone, stage, lectern, screen, projector]?

Will this be in [the auditorium, the conference room, your office, my office]?

May I see the [room, space] ahead of time?

I would like to check the equipment thirty minutes before the meeting.

*I will send out my **PowerPoint** slides the day before.*

*I will have **takeaways**.*

Could someone please make photocopies of my [presentation, handouts]?

Steps to Prepare Your Presentation
1. Think of the topic you want to talk about.
2. Write an outline focusing on the main topics you want to include.
3. Write down your entire presentation.
4. Create index cards of the main points of the presentation, which you can use to trigger your memory, rather than reading your presentation.
5. Perform the presentation multiple times in front of a mirror and, then, for another person.
6. Record the presentation, which gives you the opportunity to hear yourself and to time your presentation.

*****Culture Hints:*** *Presentations are difficult enough without being surprised about the room, the audience, and other factors that you could have known about in advance. Therefore, it is in your best interest to find out every detail prior to your presentation.*

*As companies cut costs, they often turn to **virtual presentations** in order to save travel and other expenses. This non-face-to-face presentation has its own special worries, including whether all the attendees have the correct equipment to "attend" and if the presentation is during all attendees' work hours (time zones). Other concerns include all the factors that apply to a face-to-face presentation (voice, dress, and so on).*

Idioms and Other Vocabulary

CEO: Chief Executive Officer
Coach: to teach, train, help
Dirty, off-color, or blue jokes: jokes with dirty language or images
Flattered: pleased with praise
Flip chart: large tablet of paper on an easel used for casual brainstorming and taking notes during a meeting
Jog memories: refresh memory; remind
Jokes: clean joke with no dirty language or images used
Jump into it: just do it
Lie: untruth (A white lie, or fib, is a small, usually harmless, lie. Bullshit, also referred to as B.S., is absolute nonsense and is an inappropriate phrase to use on the job.)
Make a good impression: to give favorable influence
Networking events: events where you meet new people and exchange ideas
PowerPoint: a popular software program that enables the user to present ideas in a series of slides
Pronouncing: forming words, producing words
Pronunciation: the manner of pronouncing or forming words (The distinctions between the verb *pronounce* (pronouncing) and the noun *pronunciation* are often troublesome because of the similarity in meaning and the difference in spelling.)
Skim: look through quickly
Takeaways: prepared pages or information for attendees to take after attending a presentation or talk
Tent cards: cardboard cards pre-folded in half and placed on a table in front of the speakers, usually with the speakers' names on them

Virtual presentation: a presentation given on the computer, on the Web, online, or over a conference call—in other words, not face-to-face

White board: a white surface that can be written on, used in a classroom and usually placed on the wall; often a casual brainstorming tool

Won't hurt: might help you

Chapter 14

How to Say It

People say that one of the greatest fears is the fear of speaking in public. As a matter of fact, there is a joke often told about this: "People are so much more afraid of speaking in front of a group than of dying that at a funeral they would rather be the **corpse** than the person who has to give the **eulogy**."

Nervousness about public speaking is natural even for trained speakers. You can use this anxiety constructively to help you prepare your presentation and yourself. First, get as much information as you can about the presentation.

Phrases to Introduce Yourself

[Hello, Hi, Good morning, Good afternoon, Good evening], I am (your name).

I represent (your company, your department).

My company is _____.

I work at _____.

*I am the [production manager, **VP** of sales, pharmaceutical rep].*

Thank you for [inviting me to speak, having me here, asking me to speak].

I am [glad, happy, delighted] to be here.

I have heard so much about you.

I want to talk about . . .

My topic is . . .

My [talk, presentation] is about . . .

I would like to address the issue of . . .

It is so nice to meet you.

*It is a pleasure to [**stand before you** now, be here, join you, have been invited to speak].*

*Let me tell you a little bit about [me, my background, my background as it **pertains to** this presentation, my background as it relates to this presentation].*

Phrases for Emphasis During a Presentation

It is often helpful for your listeners to allow a mental break, a pause, and then a summary of what you've said up to that point. Preface special points you want to make with these phrases:

Let me repeat that.

This is an important point.

I want to emphasize . . .

I can't emphasize enough . . .

This is the key.

Let me summarize some essential points.

Let me draw your attention to . . .

Listen to this.

And finally . . .

Closing Phrases

Thank you for your [attention, kindness, participation, consideration, time].

It has been [wonderful, a pleasure, great] to have this [opportunity, chance, occasion] to discuss this [matter, subject, problem, issue] with you.

I [look forward to, anticipate, hope to have the opportunity] to speak with you again on this and related [matters, subjects, problems, issues].

*Thank you for your attention. If you have any **feedback** or questions, I would love to hear it.*

Please e-mail me any further thoughts you have.

Before the actual presentation, take several deep breaths, and relax your facial muscles by yawning. Choose two people in the audience, one to your right and one to your left; gradually glance from one to the other while speaking.

Speak slowly and clearly, more slowly than you would speak in your native language. **Enunciate**, giving special attention to **complete word production**; don't drop the ends of words. Pause briefly between words, especially before and after names, numbers, and words with which you have particular difficulty. Additionally, stress important words, project your voice to the back of the room, and pay attention to your body language.

Culture Hint: *Know that your audience wants you to succeed; they are **rooting for** you. They are with you and want to learn from you.*

Idioms and Other Vocabulary

Complete word production: saying the entire word without dropping syllables, especially the ends of words

Corpse: dead body

Enunciate: pronounce clearly

Eulogy: speech at a funeral

Feedback: comments or advice

Pertains to: has to do with, concerning

Rep: short for *representative*

Rooting for: hoping you succeed

Stand before you: appear in front of you

VP: vice president

Chapter 15

Answering Questions

People will undoubtedly have questions to ask, even in a small group. Always ask for questions after your presentation. If no one asks a question, you could say, "Some of you may be wondering about . . ." After a question is asked, repeat or restate it. This will help those who may not have heard the question as well as ensure that you under-stand the question. Repeating the question also gives you time to think about the answer. Answer questions in as few words as you can; do not start a second presentation.

The most **seasoned** speaker gets **thrown by** inquiries. Prepare in advance by practicing what you plan to say and thinking of questions you may be asked. Also, practice in front of associates, colleagues, or friends, and have them bring up their suggestions so you can rehearse **fielding** questions and different techniques used to answer questions.

Phrases If You Know the Answer

The answer to the question is . . .

I [believe, think, know, am sure] that answer is . . .

I am [glad, happy, delighted, pleased] that you [brought that point up, raised that issue, questioned that development].

You raise an important point that I'm happy to address.

I'm glad you brought that up. I can answer you simply by saying . . .

Yes, I would like to [answer, address] that [question, point, issue].

Thank you for your question. The answer is . . .

Phrases for After You Answer a Question

Does that [answer, address] your question?

Is that what you [mean, are referring to, need to know, want to know]?

I [think, believe] the answer to that question is . . .

I hope that answers your question.

*Did I **adequately** address your question?*

Phrases to Clarify Questions

Remember, don't fake understanding. People will respect your authentic attempt to grasp their meaning.

Could you please [repeat that question, say that again, speak a little more loudly, speak more slowly, run that by me again]?

I am sorry, I did not [get that, hear that, understand that, follow you].

If I understand you correctly, you're asking (repeat question).

Let me see if I understand you: you're saying (repeat the question).

Could you [tell me more, explain that in more detail, expand on that]?

Would you be able to put that question in [other words, simpler terms, different language]?

Would you please [spell that name for me, repeat that name for me, spell that term for me, say that again]?

English is not my first language.

I have only been in the United States for six months.

I appreciate your patience; English is not my native language.

*Thanks for your understanding; I'm still **getting a grip** on English. Did you say (repeat)?*

Phrases If You Don't Know the Answer

Remember, don't **fake** an answer if you don't have the information. Don't pretend to know an answer. It can and probably will come back to **haunt you**.

I don't have that information [here, now, at this time, with me].

I am afraid I don't know that.

Is there anyone in the room who can answer that?

I will be glad to check it out and get back to you.

Let me get back to you on that.

Time is limited, but see me after the meeting and I will tell you what I know.

Please leave me your e-mail address, and I will send you the information.

Phrases for After a Presentation

After any presentation, you may be **mingling** with your audience. Attendees may come up to you with further questions or comments or just wishing to network.

Let's exchange e-mails so that we can discuss this further.

I can see we have lots more to talk about. Let me call you later.

I have extra handouts here.

I can send you a follow-up e-mail with more information.

Thank you for your comments during the presentation.

I wanted to address your comment more but didn't have the time. Perhaps we can talk more about it later?

Culture Hint: Be polite to questioners; don't make them feel sorry that they asked a question. Don't spend too much time on questions that are not relevant to the presentation. You may say, "The answer to your question is rather involved. I will be happy to discuss it with you after we finish." Remember to try to take questions from different sections of the audience.

Idioms and Other Vocabulary

Adequately: sufficiently, well enough

Fake: pretend

Fielding: answering

Getting a grip on: getting control of something (in this case, the English language)

Haunt you: cause problems

Mingling: informally gathering with other people at an event

Seasoned: has a lot of experience

Thrown by: overwhelmed by

Part 4 Notes Section

Part 5

Networking Within Your Organization and Beyond

"Her Product"

Oscar, an executive from Brazil, came to the United States and to Customized Language Skills Training (CLST) for a one-month immersion program in advanced ESL. He **ate, drank, and studied in English** from early morning to late at night with different instructors and was involved in many different activities.

One evening I took Oscar to a business networking meeting at a local restaurant. There, in small groups, we introduced ourselves. When it was my turn I said, "My name is Natalie Gast, and my company is Customized Language Skills Training. We design and conduct language programs in English as a Second Language (ESL), accent modification, and many foreign languages for business and industry." Oscar, who was standing next to me, was next to introduce himself. He said, "My name is Oscar. I am from Brazil, and I am her product." Everyone laughed! It was an **icebreaker** and one of the best **endorsements** CLST ever received.

Chapter 16

Whom Do You Know?

What Is a Network?

To network, a verb, has been defined as

- to meet with people in order to advance one's career
- to meet new clients, to establish relationships with colleagues
- to meet other people, either involved in the same work as you, or not, to share information or help each other
- to solicit information and opinions and aid associates with common goals

Network as a noun has been defined as

- an association of mutual interest
- a chain of interconnected people, who have a common interest
- meetings with other people involved in similar **pursuits** to share information and support each other

In the United States, networking is a prevalent way of doing business, increasing business, or building relationships within and among businesses and companies. Networking, itself, has become a large business. Examples of networking events include conventions, exhibitions, trade shows, meetings, office parties, and business meetings before or after work. The Internet offers a wide variety of networking opportunities. New networking sites appear every day. Some of these websites are for business professionals to interact with each other. Especially these days, it is important to guard personal information and remember that the Internet may not be the place to reveal any private data.

Networking involves building a group of business and personal contacts. You may meet people who cannot help you directly, but they may introduce you to other people who can. Of course, you may be able to help them and that is the first rule of building a business relationship. Give before you get! Networking is all about building relationships; the business follows. If you show an interest in other people, they are more likely to show interest in you.

Your success in networking depends on your ability to communicate and interact with other people. These meetings can be **awkward**—meeting new people, who many times have their hands filled with food, drink, papers, and business cards. There is often music in the background, and there is always noise in the room. If you find it difficult to communicate easily with other people, then you will find networking a real challenge. If, **on the other hand**, you are outgoing and enjoy meeting new people, you will **take to** networking more quickly.

The foreign born have an advantage, they may be unaware of, at networking events. They come from interesting places where Americans may have been. If people have been to your country, they may be eager to discuss the sights. If not, they may be curious. Also, in this setting, colleagues will usually be patient with your language issues, will want to help, and will admire your courage in attending a meeting at which they may be as uncomfortable as you are.

Phrases to Use Your "Unique-ness" to Your Advantage

You may have noticed, English is not my first language.

You may hear that I am not from the United States.

I am from _____.

My native language is _____.

I have been studying English for _____.

I would like to improve my conversational English—what do you recommend I do?

I have been here for [days, weeks, months, years].

This is my [first, second, tenth] time in the United States.

Have you ever been to my country? If so, what did you find most interesting?

Were you in my country for work or pleasure?

Do you travel a lot?

Where else have you been?

I have worked for (name of company) for (amount of time).

I have never been to a meeting of this type before.

I really like the format of this meeting.

Are there other groups or meetings in this area that I can attend? I want to meet more people in my field.

What can you recommend that I can do in my spare time to improve my English?

I need to buy a winter coat. I didn't expect it to be so cold this time of the year. Is there a reasonably priced store in this area to get one?

How often do you meet people from my country?

Do you know any other people from my country?

Culture Hint: In the United States, first names are most often used at networking meetings. You may be told immediately, "Please call me Bob" when Robert P. Smith is on his card and you address him as Mr. Smith. The order of most names in the United States is first name, middle name, and last name (surname). Titles include Mr., Miss (unmarried woman), Mrs. (married woman), and Ms. (pronounced Miz and used when you don't know if the woman is married or not), and Dr.

Idioms and Other Vocabulary

Ate, drank, and studied in English: immersed oneself in English

Awkward: uncomfortable

Endorsements: support or approval

Icebreaker: something said or done to make people less nervous when they first meet

On the other hand: something said when talking about opposite situations

Pursuits: activities

Take to: start to like

Chapter 17

How to Network

Even if networking is difficult for you, do it! It works, and it gets easier with practice. You can network in many settings. The most common places to network are business functions designed to bring people together just for that purpose. Chambers of Commerce and other business organizations have networking events. You should also be prepared to network any time anywhere. You might be at a child's sporting event and get into a conversation with another parent. That parent might mention a need for your product or service. Always have business cards with you. This is not the time to try to sell; just respond with a card.

What to Do

- Bring a supply of business cards. Even if it is your own company's meeting, you won't know or remember everyone there—especially if you are a new hire or visiting the United States.
- Wear clothes with pockets, if possible, and put cards you collect from others in one pocket and your cards to give out in another. Don't mix them up!

- Leave at least one hand free to shake hands and to exchange cards.
- When you find time during the event or soon after (before you forget), write notes on the backs of the cards you receive. Here are some sample notes to write on business cards you collect:
  - Best time to call is early A.M.
  - Needs info on Japan, wants to go in January
  - Wants to meet before next week's teleconferencing call
  - From Ecuador, wants to have lunch and practice English with me
  - In the printing business, call for quote
- Introduce yourself and others to new people who join the group. It is a good way to practice the new names you've learned.
- When speaking in a small group, try to face the door and have your listeners face in the other direction. That way, they can pay more attention to you and not focus on people coming into the room. You should focus on your listeners and not **glance** around the room.
- Before joining a conversation in progress, look and listen quietly. You wouldn't want to interrupt by adding something inappropriate. If the group doesn't **open up** to accept you, when there is a **lull** in the conversation you may be able to introduce yourself and **dovetail** into what the group has been speaking about (e.g., "I'd like to hear more about your ideas on this issue").

If you are going to remain in the United States for a considerable length of time, **make it a point** to repeat visits to networking events of the same organization in order to build relationships. People like to do business with people they know.

What Not to Do

- Talk about yourself and your business *only*.
- Act **pushy** by concentrating on only selling.
- Interrupt others; instead let others finish their thoughts or words.

Introductory Phrases to Say

Hello, I am (your name).

Hi, my name is _____. And your name?

My name is _____. Everyone calls me (nickname, first name).

I work in a similar [department, division] at my company.

Do you live in the city proper?

Do you telecommute?

Do you work in a home office or at the headquarters?

How often do you come into the main office?

I work in a satellite office.

I work out of my home.

What business are you in?

What do you do at (company)?

How long have you worked at (company)?

Do you travel a lot in your position?

I have heard [a lot, nothing, very little] about your company. Tell me [more, what I may not know].

I work at _____ as a _____.

I am here for a year from (branch) in (country).

I am interning in the department.

Our company is very active in _____.

Networking Phrases

Use questions to break the ice. Open-ended questions are better than yes or no questions because they encourage conversation.

What do you like best about working in the pharmaceutical industry?

Why did your company choose this Chamber of Commerce?

Do you enjoy telecommuting?

What do you enjoy at this meeting?

What types of businesses are usually at these meetings?

This is my first meeting of this group.

Are you a member and if so for how long?

Americans like to talk about the weather, sports, travel, entertainment, and family. It is best to avoid talking about politics, religion, salary, age, and appearance.

Phrases for Clarification

Where is your location? I am not from the United States.

Did I understand you to say that you sell books?

Excuse me, could you please repeat that?

I missed that, would you mind saying it more slowly, please?

I didn't catch that, could you say it again, please?

You did say you are traveling to Japan next week, didn't you?

How is that teleconference next month going to work?

Would you mind spelling that for me, please?

Phrases to Give Opinions

I think that . . .

In my opinion . . .

I believe . . .

I suppose . . .

Phrases to End a Conversation

It was very nice meeting you.

I hope to see you at another meeting.

I'm sorry, but I have to leave now.

I'm afraid I have to go now.

I really enjoyed talking to you.

I'll call you about . . .

Perhaps we may be able to help each other in the future.

I would like to hear more about exactly what you do, but it's a little noisy in here. May I call you in a couple of days to discuss your business further?

I want to check in with my colleague over there before she leaves. Please excuse me.

Culture Hint: *The purpose of networking meetings is to meet and interact with as many people as possible. Therefore, don't feel rejected when someone speaks to you for a short period of time, excuses himself or herself, and moves on to talk to someone else.*

Idioms and Other Vocabulary

City proper: the actual city within its boundaries, not including outlying areas, which would be "greater [name of city]" (The phrase "Chicago proper" only includes the city, not the surrounding suburbs.)

Dovetail: to fit perfectly to together

Glance: to look at quickly

I didn't catch that: I didn't hear or understand that

Lull: a short period of time when things are calm

Make it a point: make it a priority

Nickname: a shorter or different name from someone's or some place's given name (Robert may have the nickname of Bob, Bobby, Rob, or Robbie. New York is called the Empire State, and New York City is called "The Big Apple.")

Open up: stop what they are doing to allow you in

Pushy: aggressive

Satellite office: not the main office, but connected to the same company, a branch office somewhere other than where the main office is

Chapter 18

Follow-Up

Networking is not only a social activity; it involves building relationships in a social setting. This is *especially important for you*. It widens your circle of acquaintances within your organization and beyond it. You can meet people in related work ventures and others who may indirectly help you. Beyond your career, you want to find activities that you enjoyed in your country, such as cricket, snooker, soccer, darts, bocci, or curling. You may also want to find new activities that are popular in the United States. In addition, to improve and practice your American English language skills, ask your newfound acquaintances to suggest training programs, classes, or **meet-up groups**, or just to **converse** with you.

Phrases to Further Relationships

*It was nice talking to you at the sales conference. Let's do it again sometime. I have some ideas to **run past you**.*

I think we can help each other out with this project. Why don't we meet in my office to discuss it?

Let's work together on that [report, project, task].

*What do you think about **collaborating** on that project?*

Would you like to arrange a meeting at your office or mine to discuss our common business interests?

I'd like to help you on that [project, report, meeting, task].

I'd love to discuss that more and practice my English-speaking skills—how about lunch this week? I would appreciate it.

Are there any meetings you can recommend that I attend?

My wife and I are looking for a [preschool, nanny, real estate agent, language class, math tutor]. Can you help me find one?

I think I can help you. I just met the office furniture buyer in my company. Would you like his phone number?

Do you know where I can find a [cricket club, badminton court, soccer field]?

Idioms and Other Vocabulary

Collaborating: working together
Converse: talk
Meet-up groups: groups that are advertised online and get together to pursue a common interest
Run past you: tell you about

Part 5 Notes Section

Part 6

Stress at Work

Miscommunication

Marta came from Germany to her multinational company's northeast U.S. office. Since her company agreed to pay for her to come and stay in the United States, she thought she would be working in the U.S. office. Her company in Germany arranged for her to take English classes and agreed to **foot the bill** for these classes. When she reported to the site on the first day, however, the manager showed her to a cubicle with a desk, a phone, and a computer. He said, "Make yourself at home." That was the last time anyone communicated with Marta about her job. While she thought she was being sent here to work for the U.S. office, the company in Germany was **under the impression** that she wanted to combine her vacation with seeing the U.S. facility. People in the U.S. office thought Marta needed a place to work independently while visiting the country.

Marta suffered a great deal of stress because neither the German nor the American branches of her company clarified what was expected of her. She was also partly responsible for the stressful situation because she had not asked precisely what was expected of her.

Marta found herself in a foreign country with a lot of **spare time** trying to make herself understood. She had studied English as a Foreign Language (EFL) in Germany for years before coming to the United States. She was a fast learner and was among the best students in her EFL classes. She felt tremendous stress when she realized how different it is to use a foreign language with native speakers in a foreign country. People had trouble understanding her accent and regularly misunderstood her. She had difficulty understanding native English speakers as well. She found that they spoke too fast for her, but she felt embarrassed about constantly asking people to slow down.

Marta could not wait to go back to Germany and leave this difficult trip behind. If she would have stayed longer than a month, she would have **adjusted** to her surroundings and would have learned to use American English. It can be quite stressful to a person to be in a foreign country even if he or she knows the language. It takes time to **acclimate** to new people, new circumstances, and a different culture. With time, when one gets accustomed to the culture and the language, it can become an exciting adventure to be in a foreign country. Instead, misunderstandings and communication difficulties as well as change caused Marta a great deal of stress.

False Expectations

An executive from Japan was in the United States for an extended period of time. Although he had a rented car for travel to his office, which was close by, and for other short trips, he needed to take public transportation for other travel. He asked me for the book that included the schedules of all transportation in the area. I was **stunned, to say the least**. I told him that there was no book. I could get him train schedules, bus schedules, air travel information, and, probably, **ferry** information. I asked him where he heard about this "book." He said that there was such a book in his country and that it was very helpful. I thought to myself, "If there were this type of book here, we would have to **edit it frequently**." He took public transportation often, causing himself—and us—a great deal of stress. Additionally, when buses or trains were late, he had very little patience for the lack of **adherence** to the "schedule of the day."

Chapter 19

What Is Stress?

Stress is mental or physical tension or a feeling of urgency or pressure. Because you have come to the United States from a foreign country, you must expect to encounter stress. Stress can result from change in culture, language, climate, surroundings, work, or even actual dangers. Extreme stress can lead to **burnout** and also become a serious health problem.

Recognizing stress is the first step to alleviating it. The issue may not be **black and white**. Culture shock is certainly a part of the stress equation for the foreign born. "Language shock" is sometimes overlooked. Many advanced English as a Second Language/English as a Foreign Language (ESL/EFL) learners have studied English in their countries. They read, write, speak, and understand the English language . . . in their countries. When these learners try to function in English in the United States, however, they experience the shock of thinking that they must have learned a language other than English. Skill-related stress enters here because these people are now called upon to perform in English, and at a high level. Studying English in your native country and using the language on the job in the United States involve very different skills. The language learners may even be asked to close a deal or make a presentation in English; think about the stress involved!

Phrases to Ask Yourself to Determine If You Are Overstressed

Do I have enough time, patience, or knowledge to do this task?

Do I have [the language, enough English, the proper English] to do this and to do it in the time frame given?

Am I worried about being interrupted?

Am I losing focus or concentration?

I seem to be losing [focus, concentration]; can we take a break?

*Do I have to learn a new skill to **handle** this task?*

*Does this task require more people to **tackle it**?*

*What else is **on my plate**?*

Do I have to work together with someone else?

Is my colleague stressed?

Is my boss [stressed, angry, worried, impatient, overloaded with work]?

How will this change my schedule?

*How will this **impact on** the other work I'm doing?*

Will I have time to [eat lunch, complete my other work, accept phone calls, take breaks to exercise, use my vacation time]?

Will I have to work overtime?

May I ask for an extension?

My schedule is already so [packed, full, loaded, overloaded].

Some stress is beneficial and can often help people perform better in certain situations. An actor about to go on the stage has to have his or her **lines** and movements memorized, and a concert violinist must know all of the **fingering**, notes, and cues. **Harnessing** stress and balancing the tension is always helpful in situations such as these. The results are far better than if these performers were totally relaxed or overstressed. There is, however, a fine line between valuable stress and destructive stress.

Culture Hint: People from other countries often say that Americans live to work and people from other countries work to live. In many cases, this seems to be true. Americans have less vacation time than those in many other countries. If it is offered, Americans will often trade their vacation time for extra money. In unsettled business times many who have jobs hesitate to take vacations, many who are looking for work don't want to miss a possible job opportunity while traveling, and even top management feels the need to be on the job.

Even for those who do take a vacation, many take their electronic devices with them in order to be available or stay connected.

Idioms and Other Vocabulary

Acclimate: to become used to
Adherence: following a rule
Adjusted: made changes to fit in

Black and white: clear-cut

Burnout: the feeling of always being very tired

Edit it frequently: correct it many times

Ferry: a boat that takes people and vehicles back and forth

Fingering: placement of the fingers of the left hand on the strings of a stringed instrument

Foot the bill: pay the bill

Handle: take care of, do, complete

Harnessing: taking control of

Impact on: have an effect on

Lines: words that an actor says in a play

On my plate: on my schedule

Spare time: free time, leisure time

Stunned: shocked

Tackle it: work on it, make an effort to work on a job, with the sense that the job or task is difficult (a football idiom)

To say the least: the simple version (There is a more detailed way to say something, but this is the simplest way to say it.)

Under the impression: to believe that something is true

Chapter 20

Use the Good Stress

Harness the feeling of needing to **alleviate** the stress by coming up with specific techniques to do just that.

The common wisdom is that people who eat well, exercise, and have a positive outlook are not only healthier but are more productive. Following are steps you can take to strengthen your stress resistance.

- Plan your diet so you are not making last-minute decisions and choosing the wrong foods.
- Avoid food shopping when you are hungry; you buy more junk food when your stomach is empty.
- Look for nutritious choices in the company cafeteria or local restaurant.
- Don't feel like you have to eat something that you don't really want to eat because others are eating it.

Phrases for Eating Healthful Foods and Avoiding Unhealthful Foods

*I'll **pass on** the pasta and garlic bread; I find that a high **carb** lunch makes me tired and unfocused in the afternoon.*

Why don't we offer fruit along with the sweets at our staff meetings?

I found these really healthy snacks in my local grocery, would you like to try one?

I'd love to join you. Does that pizza place offer salads too?

*I won't allow my children to eat what I consider **junk foods.***

Sorry, my best wishes are with you, but I'll have to say no to the birthday cake.

May I have the dressing on the side, please?

Can you substitute a vegetable for the potatoes?

Thanks for offering a [fat-free, vegetarian, non-dairy, low-calorie] choice for dinner.

Exercising

- Walk at lunchtime.
- Use stairs instead of elevators.
- Park farther away from your entrance.
- Do isometrics and stretching exercises at your desk.
- Join a gym, hire a personal trainer, or buy a treadmill or an exercise bicycle, if your budget allows for these.
- Wake up earlier and exercise with TV exercise programs or go for a run or power walk before leaving for work.

Phrases for Exercising

*I'm going to have a **quick bite** and take a walk. Join me?*

I'll see you at the meeting. I'm going to take the stairs.

I don't mind standing, thank you. Let someone else have this seat.

I usually park at the far end of the parking lot. Would you like me to drop you off at your car?

Do you want to see what I learned at the gym today? It will only take ten minutes.

Mental Exercising

- **Visualize** yourself in a favorite place in your country.
- Visualize yourself in a nice place you have visited in the United States.
- Visualize yourself succeeding at a difficult task **such as** making a presentation.
- Get up, walk to the window, and look outside.
- Take a short break and talk to a coworker, your supervisor, or yourself (very quietly).

Phrases to Say to Yourself to Relax

*I need to take a break and **clear my head**.*

Take a deep breath.

Calm down.

Breathe deeply and focus.

*Let's just concentrate on the **task at hand**.*

I'm now looking at the [mountains, ocean, bazaar, Capitol, park].

I'm [walking along the beach, walking in the park, looking at the Golden Gate Bridge, looking at the Washington Monument].

I'll soon be saying, "Thank you all for your enthusiastic response to my presentation."

I just have to look at the park outside for a few more minutes before facing that report.

Culture Hint: America is a solution-oriented and goal-oriented society, and a certain amount of stress or tension forces us to solve problems and make decisions. It is difficult to make **across-the-board** life changes all at once. Therefore, prioritizing and looking at one aspect of the stress issue, making changes there, and congratulating yourself for that progress before moving to the next area of change, is a low-stress way to handle change.

Idioms and Other Vocabulary

Across-the-board: affecting everything
Alleviate: ease
Carb: short for *carbohydrate*
Clear my head: be able to think clearly, remove other than relevant thoughts from my head
Junk foods: foods with fat and/or sugar but no healthful nutritional value
Pass on: say no to

Quick bite: something small to eat that can be eaten in a short time

Such as: like, similar to

Task at hand: needs attention *now;* the job that has top priority; the job that is right in front of you

Visualize: imagine, see in your mind

Chapter 21

Lose the Bad Stress

When a task is overwhelming to you, break it up into manageable parts. Then, only concentrate on one part at the time. This will reduce the stress on you.

Another way to reduce your stress is to increase your exercise regimen. Everybody is different. Some people like to exercise in the morning, and some at the end of the day. Find the ideal time for you.

Don't push yourself beyond what you can do effectively or let others push you to that point. Learn to set limits.

Phrases to Help Reduce Your Stress

I'd like to do this, but I will need some extra time to [do it correctly, finish it to my or your satisfaction].

Yes I can, once I complete . . .

Please give me until [this afternoon, tomorrow, next week].

I want to help, but I'll have to call you back [in an hour, tomorrow, Monday].

What is the [deadline, timeline] on this project?

Please send me an e-mail with the specifics.

I'd like to include your information, but my deadline is tomorrow.

John, can you please help Mrs. Smith? She needs . . .

Monique will help you . . .

We need a team meeting to determine responsibility.

Culture Hints: Sometimes it is necessary to request a delay in the completion of a project or the performance of one's job. Additionally, sometimes people **bite off more than they can chew.**

Americans sometimes forget that you are often thinking in your native language and may need additional time to translate your thoughts. In a one-to-one conversation, you may be honest and tell the other person. This can de-stress both of you. Instead of your colleague, acquaintance, manager, or other person trying to figure out—from your facial expressions—whether or not you understand him or her, you will both be involved in an honest, meaningful conversational situation. A phrase to use to approach this situation could include: "I need a little more time to [understand, process, think about] what you have said before [answering you, giving you my answer, replying to your question]."

There will always be pressures and stress in work and other areas of your life. Don't think that you are the only one dealing with these issues. In the United States, stress reduction is a major subject. More and more companies offer seminars to deal with this. Those who have moved here from other countries have an added layer of stress; living in a foreign country can be very stressful. You may be happy in the United States but still miss your family, your country, your language, and your customs. This is called being homesick. Homesick is when you miss your *connections at home. Communicate regularly with your family and friends in your country by phone and e-mail. Also, continue practicing your native customs while in the United States. Learn and speak English as much as you can, but also retain your native language ability.*

Idioms and Other Vocabulary

Bite off more than they can chew: to try to do more than they are able to do

Part 6 Notes Section

Part 7

Directions

Workout at the Jim?

My husband and I were getting into our car in a parking lot when a man rushed up to us and asked, "How do you spell *Jim*?" My husband replied, "J-I-M." I, the English as a Second Language teacher, asked, "Why, are you writing to someone named Jim?" The man had a puzzled look on his face and he said, "No, I don't know Jim; my job is to paint a sign on that building," he said as he pointed to the deteriorating sign on the door of Bally's, a popular fitness center company in the United States.

We realized then the "gym" he meant. I explained that *gym* is short for *gymnasium* and the other *Jim* is the man's name, Jim. "Didn't they write it down for you?" I asked. "No," he said. My husband continued, "When did you start this job?" "This morning," he answered. If we hadn't coincidentally met in that parking lot, he probably would have proudly painted "Jim" on the door to Bally's gymnasium.

Chapter 22

Directions on the Job

Directions **permeate** every area of our lives:

- Telling someone how to perform a task or job
- Understanding when someone tells you to perform a task or a job
- Telling someone how to reach a location
- Finding out from someone how to reach a location
- Telling someone how to make, cook, or bake something
- Learning how to make, cook, or bake something
- Taking medication safely
- Using the ever-increasing variety of technical devices

It is always **critical** to be clear when giving directions and to understand completely and accurately when following directions. When giving directions or instructions, it is very important to speak slowly and **audibly**; don't cover your mouth with your hands or with papers. Check frequently during your explanation to determine if you have been understood.

When you are taking directions, it is also valuable to check often to ensure that you have understood what you have been told. If clarity and understanding are sacrificed, you may be responsible for someone having difficulty at work or may risk performing your work inadequately. Additionally, you may cause someone to get lost or you, yourself, may get lost. You may make a terrible recipe for your family or for guests or ruin someone else's meal preparation. You may take too much or too little medication. You may have an expensive TV and not be able to use all the features. You may buy a DVD player or camera and put off using it because the directions are not clear to you.

Receiving Directions

When receiving directions, remember that Americans are uncomfortable with silence, lack of feedback, and, especially, no reaction to what they have said. A very long pause may make an American think you didn't hear, didn't understand, or are ignoring him or her. When people speak to you, they expect you to respond or react in some way. Reacting lets others know that you are listening. **Acknowledging** someone, especially when that person is giving directions to you, is important. An easy way to remember how to pay special attention to one who is giving you directions is to think about the word *react*. What does it mean to react?

R Respond
E Eye contact
A Act—ask questions
C Contribute an idea
T Turn around

What does it mean to respond? As people speak, let them know you understand with words such as: *okay, yes, I see, all right, go on, good, sure, I hear you,* and *no problem.* If you do not fully understand, respond by saying, "I don't understand." Or ask for clarification:

I'm not sure I understand . . .

Before you move on . . .

Pardon me, I have a question . . .

Could I please ask a question?

Sorry to interrupt, but you said . . .

Excuse me, but I heard you say . . .

Going back to what you said before . . .

Please repeat that more slowly . . .

Did you say . . . ?

Do you mean . . . ?

What about eye contact? It is important to make eye contact with someone who is speaking to you. It shows you are interested in what that person is saying and that you are paying attention. A good way to start out making eye contact is to notice the color of the person's eyes. You may, then, continue to look at the person's face, but do not **stare** fixedly into his or her eyes.

What does it mean to act or ask questions? When someone is giving you directions, another way to exhibit understanding is to ask questions—if you have any. "Do you mean file the reports in this file cabinet?" You may also act by walking over to the file cabinet.

How do you contribute an idea? Perhaps you have an idea or suggestion that might help. You may offer it now. "Would it work to **color-code** the files and put all the **delinquent** bills in the red file so they would be easier to find?"

Why is it important to turn around? If someone has started to speak to you, it is rude not to turn around and face the person. It is difficult to speak to someone's back; you don't know if the person hears, understands, or relates to you and what you are saying. When you turn around and face the other person, both of you can read a lot from each other's facial expressions and body language.

Phrases for Giving Directions to Others

Could you please [copy, print, download, upload, e-mail, open, close] . . . ?

*Could you possibly [give out, type, put together, **edit**, **proofread**] the [flyers, memos, mailing list, **company newsletter**]?*

*Please [put up, take down, put away, clean up, put back] the [wall calendar, clock, **white board**, **pegboard**].*

I'd like you to [check my work, give me feedback, help me out, set up a meeting, back me up].

I need you to [come early, stay late, change your schedule, cover for Paul].

Can you just do one more thing for me?

*The [boss, manager, director, owner] has asked that we [complete the project, have a conference, attend a meeting, **stagger** our lunch hours, stagger our coffee breaks].*

*Could you please [help me, **pitch in**, **give me your take on this**, **give me a hand**]?*

*This task is confusing; you may want to **jot down** a few notes.*

*When you **edit** for Mr. Monroe, please use a red pen.*

Let me demonstrate this process for you.

First, review last month's report by Jonathan.

Please interrupt me if I speak too quickly or you don't understand a step.

Everyone is required to follow the safety procedures that are posted. Let's review each of the safety procedures to ensure that everyone understands them.

*Always use the spell check and grammar check programs, but use your own **common sense** in the process. These programs often misunderstand **context**.*

Phrases to Use When Taking Directions

I'll get right on that.

No problem.

Consider it done.

I understand.

Sure.

Could you repeat that please?

Please rephrase that.

Could you clarify that?

Where would you like to meet?

What did you say you needed?

What did you mean by [changing my schedule, having meetings more frequently, coming up with a suggestion form]?

Who should get the [memo, newsletter, e-mail, notice]?

Culture Hints: *Never be shy to ask for clarification It is not* **shameful** *to ask questions. It was better for the man in the anecdote to find out how to spell* gym *before he incorrectly painted it on the sign on the door. It would have been still better if he had asked his boss to write it down for him before he was about to paint it and before he began searching for strangers in a parking lot, strangers who might have spelled it incorrectly.*

As a general rule, it is impolite to interrupt. However, when someone is giving you multiple directions, it may be necessary to stop the person for clarification before he or she finishes a long series of complex commands. When a person tells you how to do a specific job in many steps, for example:

> *First, you unload everything from the truck, including the hardware.*
>
> *Then, you unpack the boxes.*
>
> *Then, you read the directions carefully.*
>
> *And finally, you assemble the furniture.*

You may have a question or comment, for example, about the first direction; you may be thinking I didn't see any hardware. Is it in the cab of the truck instead of the back of the truck? *You may interrupt after step 1 and say, "Excuse me, I hate to interrupt, but I want to ask this question before it gets* **lost in the shuffle**.*"*

Another interesting point about directions: Don't be confused by elevators that go from the 12th to the 14th floor. In many office buildings or apartment houses, there is no "13th floor"; 13 is considered bad luck, and many don't want to live or work on the 13th floor.

Idioms and Other Vocabulary

Acknowledging: taking notice of

Audibly: loudly enough to be heard

Color-code: to designate by color

Common sense: reasoning

Company newsletter: printed report about a company's activities

Context: related words and phrases

Critical: very important

Delinquent: past due

Edit: remove mistakes from written material

Give me a hand: help me

Give me your take on this: tell me what you think about this

Jot down: write down quickly

Lost in the shuffle: forgotten in moving things around

Pegboard: a board with holes into which pegs or hooks are put to hang things on

Permeate: spread through every part

Pitch in: to help

Proofread: read for correcting errors

Shameful: really bad

Stagger: to move around so that not everything takes place at the same time

Stare: to look at for a long time without moving your eyes

White board: a white surface that can be written on, used in a classroom and usually placed on the wall; often a casual brainstorming tool

Chapter 23

Giving and Following Directions to Get Somewhere

Nowadays many new cars come with a Global Positioning System (GPS), which conveniently gives directions. You may also buy a GPS separately and add it to your car. This system has become more popular, easier to use, and less expensive. The GPS can be programmed to speak to the user in one of a number of languages. The convenience of a GPS is that you can mount it on your car's dashboard at eye level and it speaks to you when your eyes are focused on the road. People also use MapQuest and similar websites to get directions. These sites will give you step-by-step directions and a map to get from one destination to another.

Remember that there are also actual paper or plastic maps you can buy in a gas station, bookstore, or store where newspapers are sold. If you are driving, bicycling, or walking to some place and do get lost, it is best to ask for directions at a gas station, store, shopping area, or police station. When you don't know the area, ask for **landmarks**.

When giving directions to someone, it can be extremely helpful to give familiar landmarks. Some popular places include a post office, school, police station, church, fast-food restaurant, or anything that stands out on the route along the way. Landmarks can also be stop signs; traffic lights; blinking lights, or **blinkers**; one-way streets; construction sites; U-turn signs; and railroad tracks.

You may also need to have directions to get around your place of work, a store, or other building sites. Most large facilities have site maps, some even in frames in the **lobby** of the building. If you are visiting a colleague, client, or customer at a large **facility**, a guard may give you a map as you drive in. **Interior maps** may also be available.

Phrases to Use When Asking for Directions

I [am lost, am confused, need help, made the wrong turn, need directions].

[Can you tell me, Do you know] where the [post office, hospital, mall, bus station, local bank, gas station] is?

[I am trying to get to, How do I get to, Which way is, Where can I find] [Elm Street, the town post office, the town police station, the hospital, the nearest gas station, Dr. Smith's office]?

What is the [easiest, best, most direct, shortest, fastest] way to get to . . . ?

[How do I get to, Where do I find, Where is, Please direct me to, Could you please tell me where] [the elevator, the escalator, the restroom, the men's room, the ladies' room, the dressing room, the supply closet, the conference room] is?

Is the [conference room, copy center, health club] on this floor?

Phrases to Use When Giving Directions to Somewhere

Make a left at the intersection.

*It's the third exit on the right after the **toll**.*

Pass the railroad tracks, and make a left at the blinking light.

Go to the end of the hall and make a left. It's the door next to the ladies' room.

Take a left.

Make a right.

Go upstairs.

Take the stairs.

Make the third left.

Culture Hints: *Before you sit behind the wheel of a car, you should familiarize yourself with the local traffic signs and lights because they may differ from those in your country. Driving rules differ from state to state in the United States, so make sure you know them as well.*

Many companies and public facilities have their own directions available on their websites. Check before going, as these are usually the best directions. Sometimes MapQuest and other sites don't give the most direct directions.

Bus, ferry, train, and other forms of public transportation offer schedules as well. These schedules are usually available online and can be downloaded. However, these schedules can change frequently, so make sure you have the latest information.

Idioms and Other Vocabulary

Blinkers: traffic lights that go on and off

Facility: a building where a specific activity takes place, or service is provided

Interior maps: maps of the inside of a building, also called a *directory*

Landmarks: places that are easy to recognize

Lobby: a large area inside the main entrance of a public building

Toll: money paid to travel on the road

Chapter 24

Other Directions to Consider

You may have occasion at work to help someone use a piece of technical equipment. Many people who are otherwise intelligent and skillful at their jobs are thrown by using unfamiliar equipment. Following are some suggestions for giving directions for using some technical devices.

Phrases for Directions to Use a New Photocopy Machine

Put the paper here.

Don't press Start until you have selected the size and the shade of darkness that you want.

Unlike our last machine, this one collates and staples.

*Put the original **facedown**.*

If you set this button, it will go to your computer.

Press this button to find out how many copies remain before you have to change the toner cartridge.

This setting tells you how many copies you have made to date.

Press this setting to copy photographs.

Don't forget to choose the proper setting for the paper size.

*Shut off the machine and open this panel to check on a **paper jam**.*

The serial number is located here; you'll need it when calling for service.

Unlike the last machine, this can copy onto card stock.

Phrases for Directions to Use a New Computer

This is very much like the previous model.

Rather than a control button, you have a command button.

Practice using some of the icons while I watch.

*Do you know about "Control + z"? It's a **lifesaver**.*

You really have to read the manual.

Try it out and write down your questions.

We'll review your questions later.

Remember to check your spam file; often new legitimate e-mail addresses show up there.

Culture Hint: *Because many employees have used their work-place computers for personal communications, computers have mechanisms that employers use to track computer use. Always check with your employer as to permissible or nonpermissible types of websites.*

Idioms and Other Vocabulary

Facedown: print side down
Lifesaver: something that makes your job very easy
Paper jam: when a sheet or piece of copier paper fails to go through the copier and causes the machine to stall

Part 7 Notes Section

Appendix A

The American Business Culture in a Nutshell

Eye Contact

When you make eye contact, people may see you as honest, trustworthy, and interested in a conversation. When you do not make eye contact, people may see you as dishonest, shy, rude, or not interested in the conversation. Good eye contact does not mean **staring**. When you make eye contact, it is not polite to look into the person's eyes for an entire conversation without ever turning your eyes away. Staring is considered rude. When you shake people's hands, notice their eye color. This will force you to look them in the eye.

Smiling

Even on the phone, people can hear your smile in your voice. Over the phone, people might think you are sad or angry by your tone of voice. It's very difficult to sound sad or angry when you are smiling.

Handshakes

Handshakes should be firm. Weak handshakes give a poor impression. Avoid **limp noodle** or **dead fish handshakes**. However, firm handshakes should not be bone crushing (so firm that you hurt the other person's hand). Handshakes should be about one or two pumps, not more. In business, handshakes are equally correct for men and women. Sometimes, to show warmth or enthusiasm, one places a second hand on top of the other person's hand. Men often do not extend their hands to women. This is one of those times for women to take the lead.

Personal Space

Personal space is important for making people feel comfortable. Americans accept a much smaller area of personal space than Asians but may need more than many Europeans. If you stand too close, people will think you are pushy or being too personal. If you stand too far away, people will think you are distant or untrusting. When standing face-to-face with someone, stand one to two feet away (arm's length). Keep cultural comforts in mind when shaking hands; don't be offended if someone from a culture different from yours either steps into the handshake or steps back to leave more space. Avoid touching the other person except for the handshake. Touching makes some people uncomfortable. Lean toward the other person to show interest. When standing side by side or sitting, the personal space will often be less than arm's length. Often, Americans give casual kisses. This occurs in social situations. In business situations, this can be inappropriate. It can cause discomfort for those not used to "casual intimacy."

Silence

Americans are not comfortable with silence. A very long pause may make an American uncomfortable. Conversations should have a constant flow, from one person to the next. When people speak to you, they expect you to respond or react in some way. Reacting lets them know that you are listening. As people speak, let them know you understand with words such as *okay, yes, I see, all right, go on, good*, or *sure*. If you do not understand, respond by saying, "I don't understand" or ask for clarification. "Please [repeat that, say that again, say that in another way, tell me if this is correct]."

Business Cards

Giving out your business cards helps people remember who you are and what you do. In the United States, we do not give out our business cards right when we walk into a meeting. We give our business cards while we are talking to people about what we do, when people ask for cards, when other people give us their cards, or at the end of a meeting when we are saying good-bye.

Appearance

"Clothes make the man" is an American expression. This means that people judge you by how you dress. Dress appropriately for the business in which you work. Standard business dress for men is a suit and tie. In more casual businesses, neat casual clothes are fine. Women wear suits, dresses, or slacks. While slacks have become acceptable for women, some corporate cultures do not accept them. Business advisors say to dress for the job you want rather than the one you have. A neat, clean appearance shows that you care about yourself and your job. Styles change and different companies have different dress codes. The American business climate is always changing. Bright colors are now standard business dress. Many companies have "dress-down" days. On these days, everyone wears casual clothes—even jeans.

Time

American culture is very aware of time. We say "time is money" and "a stitch in time saves nine" because we are careful not to waste time. People who are punctual make a good impression. Meetings should begin and end on time. If you are going to be late for a meeting or appointment, call as soon as possible to explain and apologize. You may have to reschedule. A 9:00 A.M. meeting begins at 9:00 sharp. You may arrive early to network (talk to and catch up with people).

If your culture is one that does not "jump right into" business, the American style may seem unfriendly to you. It's not. You may also note impatience among your American colleagues if things don't move along quickly. Of course, we are not a homogeneous country. Northerners are impatient with **laid-back**. Southerners can't understand the **frantic** pace of the North. Midwesterners are a **breath of fresh air** with their warmth and friendliness. So, as you try to adapt to our cultures, realize that we are adapting as well.

Management Style

Unlike many other cultures in which there is a single management style, in America there are many management styles. This can be confusing. Your current manager may be goal oriented and your next manager may be detail oriented. Follow the leader and pay attention to his or her style.

Initiative

Employers value people with initiative. Someone who waits to be told what to do at every step is thought to be less motivated than someone who is a self-starter and works with less supervision. Managers will give more responsibility to the self-starter than the person who needs to be told what to do at every step.

Equality

Americans are proud of the belief that all people are created equal. While all people may not be treated equally, we strive toward that ideal in our communities and in business. Although people are aware of levels within a company, most people work comfortably with people at different levels. Use of first names in business is common, even between supervisor and employee. Formal address (Dr., Mr., Mrs., Miss, Ms.—pronounced *Miz*) is used during a first meeting but is usually quickly replaced with first names. Follow the leader—your colleague may say, "Please call me John." Or just begin by using your first name. Men and women are given equal respect and work at all levels within organizations.

Down to Business

Americans like to get right down to business. While to some cultures that may seem rude, Americans believe that time should not be wasted. In meetings, small talk is kept to a minimum. If someone comes from another location to attend a meeting, he or she may be asked how the trip to the meeting site was. Personal information should be avoided during business meetings. Sometimes people who have been doing business for a long time may ask general questions such as, "How is the family?" These questions will be reserved for before or after the meeting. Some people are all business—respect their privacy. Other people like the personal touch and welcome questions.

It is important to understand the separation of business and personal lives. Americans tend to see work as a means of earning money. Usually there is not the sense of the company as a family as there is in some cultures. Even at "social" business gatherings, conversation tends not to get too personal and often revolves around business. Safe topics of conversation are sports and other leisure activities. These are considered small talk, which is short, friendly conversation about something that is not too personal.

Parties

When invited to an office party or any business or personal event, it's important to be clear when answering. "Yes, I'll be able to come" or "I'm sorry, I can't attend" are direct responses. In some cultures, it's rude to say no directly, even if you know you won't be able to attend. But Americans prefer a clear answer so they can plan.

Sometimes holiday parties include a "grab bag." This means that everyone brings a small, wrapped gift (usually $5 or $10). At the party, everyone chooses a gift or picks a number.

Sometimes the party is for someone. It may be a retirement or a new baby. Someone may collect money, usually just a few dollars, from everyone to buy one nice gift. Everyone signs one card. If you have a special relationship with that person, you may want to give your own card, as well. If a lot of events come at once, you may find yourself giving more money than you want to. It's awkward not to contribute: however, if it's really a problem, talk to the person collecting the money. No one wants a party to be **a hardship** on anyone.

The Alphabet of Business

A, B, C piles
ASAP
A to Z
Plan B
ETA
ETD

FYI
P's and Q's
Q and A
SOP
TBD

A, B, C Piles

Many time-management books and courses recommend dividing those papers on your desk into A, B, and C piles. The A pile contains urgent items that require immediate action. The B pile contains important items that need attention, but not immediately. The C pile contains low-priority items. Often if you ignore that C pile long enough it becomes **trash**. Many experts say that the C pile should just go directly into the trash; however, some low-priority items still must be done, if there is time.

ASAP

This is a confusing direction. It means "as soon as possible." Usually, the person making the request means now, or even "yesterday." The person receiving the request usually focuses on the word *possible*, which could mean anything from "I'll do it when I finish this task" to "I'll do it **when I get around to it**." If you really want something quickly, your best option is to say, **specifically**, by when it's needed.

A to Z

This phrase describes the full range, or, to use a few other idioms: **soup to nuts** or **the whole ball of wax**. For example, if you are trying to resolve a problem, you may say you want "every possible solution from A to Z."

Plan B

Most people plan on a particular action, take it, and move on. Some-times, taking that action becomes impossible. The idiom Americans use is "Let's go to Plan B." Another way to say this is "Our original plan won't work. We need another option." It's a good idea to have a Plan B in mind just in case you need it.

ETA and ETD

Transportation acronyms, ETA and ETD mean "estimated time of arrival" and "estimated time of departure," respectively. While they are still used for transportation, they are also used more informally. You may be waiting for someone who is typically late for meetings, and a colleague may ask, "What's his ETA?" You might be planning to leave with a colleague to meet with a client and be unsure of the schedule and ask, "What's our ETD?"

FYI

These letters mean "for your information." You may just want to keep someone **in the loop** but not want any action from that person. Often FYI is used at the top of a memo or an e-mail.

P's and Q's

Mind your p's and q's means "to behave appropriately or to dem-onstrate good manners." Here are two of the possible origins. Seventeenth-century bartenders watched how much their patrons **consumed**, noting the number of pints and quarts they drank. The bartenders suggested that patrons "mind their p's and q's." Another story refers to old printing presses, in which an upside down *p* or *q* could cause a misspelling, thus leading to the printer's caution to "mind their p's and q's."

Q and A

This phrase means "question and answer." A Q and A period often follows a lecture. A speaker may suggest that audience members save their questions for the Q and A. (Note that there's also QA, or "quality assurance"—the test by which products are assessed for final problems.)

SOP

The acronym SOP stands for "Standard Operating Procedure." For technical jobs, SOPs outline the necessary steps. Informally, SOP means "That's how we do it here."

TBD

The acronym TBD means "to be determined." You may have a project plan, but certain **benchmark** dates aren't yet firm; they might be marked TBD. You may not have decided on a final price or time frame or agenda item. These would be noted as TBD.

Words, Words, Words!

Certain general rules of conversation apply in the business world. The term "politically correct" means acceptable in a particular environment, such as your work environment. Often, those who were born in the United States and work beside you are not always as careful, or "politically correct," as they should be. You may think that because they are from this country, you can follow their example. Don't follow everyone's example, and don't follow anyone's example every time. Everyone **slips up** now and then, both in language and behavior.

Following are some guidelines that are helpful:

- **Listen.** Listening is your best asset. Listening to customers, clients, and guests helps you correctly assess their needs and respond appropriately. Listening to your manager or supervisor saves you time, and often, embarrassment from misunderstandings. Listening to colleagues and coworkers helps you work more effectively together. Finally, listening demonstrates interest and caring.

- **Summarize.** Both those with whom you work and your customer (or client) base are increasingly diverse. Summarizing requests or instructions can help all involved get the correct result; for example: "I hear you saying that . . . , is that correct?" "Is that what you meant?" "So you think that I should . . . ?" "Did I understand you to say . . . ?" "Let's summarize what we just discussed." "Let's clarify our respective roles in this project so that there isn't any **duplication of effort**."

- **Don't interrupt.** Interrupting is considered rude, but sometimes it is necessary. You may have to interrupt someone who is on the phone or in a conversation with another because you have an urgent message. Try phrases like: "I'm sorry to interrupt but . . . ," "Excuse me, may I have a moment, please?," or "Please call me as soon as you're through; something important has come up." Sometimes, conversations are a rapid exchange of information and ideas and seem to be one interruption after another. Use your judgment to determine whether or not **jumping in** is appropriate.

- **Ask questions.** Asking questions shows that you are listening and interested. Sometimes, just the right question can save everyone a lot of time. It's always better to ask than to guess and, perhaps, do the wrong thing.

- **Choose your words.** Some words and phrases may be okay in personal situations but not in business. Others just **don't cut it** in any situation. Following are phrases to avoid on the job:

Don't Say	Do Say
No, I'm busy.	*I'm sorry. I'm busy now. Can I [get back to you, do it, help you] [in ten minutes, in an hour, tomorrow]?*
This is impossible!	*This is difficult, but we'll get it done.*
	Let's think this through.
	Let's look at our options.
We don't sell that. We don't do that.	*I'm sorry, but we don't [carry that item, offer that service], but you can try our _____; it [has the same ingredients, does the same thing, is quite good]. Let me [tell you about it, show it to you, give you some samples].*
That's not my job.	*Let me get someone who can help you with that.*
Can I help you, lady?	*Can I help you?*
	Can I help you, [ma'am, miss]?
I'm out of here.	*I'll see you tomorrow.*
	Enjoy your evening.
What a dumb idea.	*That's interesting. Let's think it through.*
Speak up!	*I'm sorry; I couldn't hear you.*
Can't you see I'm busy?	*I'm sorry; I'm trying so hard to finish this. Can we talk later?*

145

Also, remember there are so many words in the language; it is unnecessary and wrong to use curse words, swear words, or bad language. Some of these words were used in our anecdotes (e.g., bullshit, B.S.) because they actually were used and the stories happened that way. They are not examples of appropriate language.

Idioms and Other Vocabulary

A hardship: a difficulty
Benchmark: standard
Breath of fresh air: something different and good
Consumed: eaten or drunk
Don't cut it: are wrong; won't work
Duplication of effort: two people doing the same work that is meant only for one to do
Frantic: hurried and, often, worried
In the loop: included and informed about what is going on
Jumping in: interrupting
Laid-back: relaxed
Limp noodle or **dead fish handshakes:** weak handshakes
Slips up: makes a mistake
Soup to nuts or **the whole ball of wax:** everything
Specifically: exactly
Staring: looking fixedly
Trash: garbage
When I get around to it: whenever I have time

Appendix B

Sports Idioms and Expressions

People in the United States play, watch, and enjoy many sports, even the less-familiar ones. Sports idioms and expressions are used in everyday conversations and in business. The following are just some of the very many examples of sports idioms and expressions used in business or personal life.

Phrases from Baseball

Touch base: Whenever a batter reaches any base, he must touch that base. In business or personal life, it means to contact someone briefly to renew an acquaintance or check on information. "I really have to touch base with my manager about the new machines."

Hit a home run: A batter hits a home run when he hits the ball so far that he can run around all the bases and reach home plate. In business or personal life, to hit a home run is to achieve the most successful outcome possible. "The new chemist is very good; I really hit a home run when I hired her."

Batting a thousand: A thousand is the most successful batting average possible. In business or personal life, this means never making a mistake. "Ivan made another sale. That's five sales and he's only been here a couple of days. He's batting a thousand."

Throw a curve: A curve is a pitch that is purposefully not thrown straight in order to confuse the batter. In business or personal life, to be thrown a curve is to be confronted with an unexpected problem. "The boss threw me a curve; he wants the report tomorrow. I thought it was due next week."

A team player: A team player performs well with the other members of his team. In business or personal life, a team player works cooperatively with other members of his or her organization. "During the job interview Human Resources asked if I was a team player. Since I like to cooperate with other people on projects, I said yes."

A ballpark figure: This is an approximation of the size of the crowd at a game. In business or personal life, it is an approximation of how much, how many, and so on. "The new office is expected to cost $20,000, but that's only a ballpark figure. It could be higher or lower."

Way off base: This occurs when a runner doesn't touch the base. In business or personal life, it is when one is very wrong about something. "I didn't want to come to the United States because I thought my English was weak, but I was way off base. I understand everyone and they understand me."

To play hardball: This is to play a very aggressive game with no thought to injury to oneself or to others. In business or personal life, it describes someone who is very competitive. "During the sales meeting, Ivan criticized every sales technique I talked about. He really plays hardball; I can't compete with him."

Rain check: If a game is called off because of rain, people use the part of the ticket they have kept to attend a future game. In business or personal life, if one cannot attend a meeting or appointment, the other person says, "I'll give you a rain check and we'll meet next week." "I had an appointment with a customer today. When he had to cancel, I gave him a rain check for Thursday or Friday."

Having two strikes against you: This is not a good position to be in whether in baseball or in business or personal life. Since there are only three strikes to strike out, having two strikes means you are almost out. "She wanted the job. However, she didn't drive, and she didn't have a babysitter for her young children. She already had two strikes against her."

Phrases from Football

Tackle: This means to bring down the running ballcarrier. In business or personal life, people tackle, attack, or confront a problem. "I'm going to tackle my taxes this weekend."

Fumble: When a player drops the ball, this mistake is called a fumble. In business or personal life, to fumble is to make a big mistake. "The salesman never asked for the order; he fumbled the opportunity to make the sale."

To run interference: This means for someone to lead the way for the ballcarrier, blocking potential tacklers. In business or personal life, it means that the person running the interference has taken care of a problem for another person. "I was so busy today that I asked my **admin** to run interference for me by putting through only the most important calls."

Touchdown: When a ballcarrier crosses the goal line and scores, it is called a touchdown, and the scoring team is awarded six points. As with "hit a home run" above, *touchdown* implies a successful outcome.

Phrases from Boxing

To be a heavyweight: A heavyweight is a boxer in the heaviest weight class; in business and personal life, a heavyweight is the most important and powerful person in the organization or in a situation. A **lightweight** is the opposite, a person who has little power. "We hired Steven because we checked his references and they all said he was a heavyweight in finance."

KO: Short for *knockout*. When a boxer KOs an opponent, the match is over. A KO can have positive and negative connotations.

Phrases from Horse Racing

To be neck and neck: Two or more horses racing evenly are said to be running neck and neck. In business or person life, two or more people who are competing evenly at a task are the same. "My sister and I are neck and neck in winning my mother's attention."

Win by a nose: When a horse wins the race by the length of a nose, it wins by a nose. In business or personal life, it refers to when one person wins by a very small margin. "My sister narrowly beat me for my mother's attention; she won by a nose."

Phrases from Tennis

The ball is in your court: This expression is used when a player has received the ball on his or her side of the net and must now make the next move. In business or personal life, this means it's up to you to make the next move. "I spoke to Jim about the job opening and told him that you would call about it. Now the ball is in your court."

Phrases from Swimming

Get one's feet wet: Instead of diving right in, some people cautiously get their feet wet first and slowly go into the water. In business or personal life, some people don't jump into a job or project, they slowly start out. "I've only been working here for three days, I've hardly gotten my feet wet."

To be drowning in something: Drowning is sinking down in the water and being unable to breathe. In business or personal life, this means drowning in work or tasks that are overwhelming. "When I volunteered for this project, I didn't realize that I'd be drowning in paperwork."

Appendix C

Grammar Notes

Contractions

Americans use contractions all the time, and they sound less formal than the non-contracted words. Contractions are used in business life as well as in personal situations to sound more natural. Whether or not you feel comfortable using contractions, it is important to be familiar with them in order to fully understand conversations with Americans. Contractions are also used widely in TV programs, movies, and music. However, in formal writing (letters, reports, and proposals) contractions are frowned upon.

Common contractions include:

I'm	you're
he's	she's
it's (*it's* can mean "it is" or "it has" depending on the context)	
we're	they're
isn't	aren't
weren't	wasn't, won't

haven't	hadn't
couldn't	shouldn't
wouldn't	mustn't
I'll	you'll
she'll	he'll
we'll	they'll
there's	

Contractions are often difficult to pronounce for nonnative speakers. Ask an American colleague, acquaintance, or friend to say them for you—maybe even record them—so that you can hear them said correctly. "Ain't" is a nonstandard English contraction for "isn't." You may hear it, but don't ever use it or write it.

Non-Rigid Pronunciation

You will certainly hear reductions, or non-rigid pronunciations, in informal situations. *Do not* use these forms in writing. Here are some examples of correct speech compared with non-rigid pronunciation in conversations. The non-rigid pronunciation is between slashes (//) under the formal pronunciation.

In an Office
John: How's your new office?
/How's yer new office?/
Pete: It's nice; how's yours?
/It's nice; how's yers?/
Would you like to see it?
/Wouldja like ta see it?/
John: Later, I have to see the boss now.
/Later, I hafta see the boss now./
Pete: What do you want to see him for?
/Whaddaya wanna see him fer?/

John: I'm waiting for a computer.
/I'm waitin' fer a computer./
He's got to get me one.
/He's gotta get me one./
He has to order it.
/He hasta order it./
I'm sort of lost without one.
/I'm sorta lost without one./

In a Factory

Steve: What are you working on?
/Whacha working on?/

Paul: I don't know. I should have read the directions.
/I dunno. I shudda read the directions./

Steve: Do you need a wrench or a screwdriver?
/Do ya need a wrench er a screwdriver?/

Paul: I'm going to look for the directions.
/I'm gonna look fer the directions./

Steve: You've got to find them soon.
/You gotta find 'em soon./

Paul: Can you help me?
/Kin ya help me?/

Steve: You must have left them home.
/You musta left 'em home./
You want a cup of coffee and think about it?
/You wanna cuppa coffee 'n think about it?/

Paul: (sneezes) Achoo!

Steve: God bless you.
/G'blesya./

Paul: He might have; here are the directions.
/He mighta; here are the directions./

In a Store

Carol: May I help you?
/May I help ya?/

Mary: Yes, I would like to buy a pair of shoes.
/Yes, I'd like tabuy apaira shoes./

Carol: What size are you?
/What sizer ya?/

Mary: 8 narrow

Carol: What color do you like?
/What color do ya like?/

Mary: I want a pair of white shoes.
/I wanna paira white shoes./

Carol: Did you want dressy or casual shoes?
/Didja want dressy or casual shoes?/
Where are you going to wear them?
/Where ya gonna wear 'em?/

Mary: To a wedding.

Carol: What color is your dress?
/What color's yer dress?/

Mary: White.

Carol: You can't wear white to a wedding!
/Ya can't wear white to a wedding!/

Mary: But I am the bride!
/But I'm the bride!/

There are many informal expressions you will hear. They include, for example, the following slang greetings:

How ya doin'?

How's it goin'?

What's doin'?

What's happenin'?

What's up?

What's new?

These could be slang answers to the greetings:

Hangin' in there.

Can't complain.

Been better.

Been worse.

Lotsa luck!

Other slang expressions include:

Chill.

Catch ya later.

Ya know?

No sweat.

No biggie.

Gotcha.

Take it easy.

Take it slow.

Phrasal Verbs

Many two- and three-word verbs are used in giving directions. They are referred to as phrasal verbs. Phrasal verbs may be separable or nonseparable. In other words, a noun or a pronoun may come between the verb and the preposition in a separable phrasal verb. They may not in a nonseparable phrasal verb.

Nonseparable

Call on: ask someone to speak (I hope the teacher doesn't call on me today.)

Catch up with: reach the same level (I couldn't catch up with Steve.)

Check into: investigate (Please check into a rented car.)

Get off: disembark from a means of transformation (We start the meeting as soon as he gets off the airplane.)

Get through: finish (I hope we get through this project by Monday.)

Get up: arise (She missed the bus because she didn't get up on time.)

Go over: review (Please go over my presentation.)

Look into: examine (Could you look into a new telephone system, please?)

Put up with: tolerate (I can't put up with this anymore.)

Run into: meet by chance (I ran into my former boss at the mall.)

Run out of: use up (You ran out of printer ink.)

Show up: arrive (The manager will show up any minute.)

Separable

Call back: return a phone call (Please call back Maria. Please call Maria back.)

Call off: cancel (I called off the meeting. I called the meeting off.)

Clear away: take things away (Please clear away the reports. Please clear the reports away.)

Cross out: delete by putting a line through it (Please cross out the last part. Please cross the last part out.)

Do over: repeat (Do over the report. Do the report over.)

Drop off: leave a thing or person somewhere (I'm sorry I'm late; I have to drop my son off at day care. I had to drop off my son at day care.)

Fill out: complete a form (I didn't fill out the application. I didn't fill the application out.)

Hand in: submit (Hand the report in. Hand in the report.)

Hang up: end a telephone conversation (Can you hang the phone up? I need to talk to you. Can you hang up the phone? I need to talk to you.)

Make something up: lie about something (He made up many things on his résumé. He made many things up on his résumé.)

Pass out: distribute (Please pass out the checks. Please pass the checks out.)

Put back: return something where it belongs (Put the files back. Put back the files.)

Scale down: make smaller or less (We are scaling down our printing expenses. We are scaling our printing expenses down.)

Slowed down: decrease the speed (The shipping department slowed the process down. The shipping department slowed down the process.)

Spill over: to overflow (He spilled the coffee over. He spilled over the coffee.)

Throw away: discard (He threw the important papers away. He threw away the important papers.)

Tie up: put together with string (You tied the package up beautifully. You tied up the package beautifully.)

About the Author

Natalie Gast brings more than thirty years' experience to language training. In 1986, she founded Customized Language Skills Training (CLST), a full-service language training company specializing in tailor-made short-term and long-term English as a Second Language (ESL) and accent reduction programs onsite in business and industry. Additionally, CLST conducts training in many foreign languages.

Customized Language Skills Training has developed industry-specific programs for foreign medical residents, engineers, bank management personnel, casino personnel, and employees of many other industries.

Gast earned her undergraduate degree at Boston University, and her master's degree work was done at Kean College, N.J. She has participated in conferences on "Responding to the Changing Economy," "Doing Business with Foreign Countries," and "Workplace Diversity." *Perfect Phrases for ESL: Everyday Business Life* is her first book. Its companion volume is *Perfect Phrases for ESL: Advancing Your Career.*

The Right Phrase for
Every Situation...Every Time